The Family Affair Cookbook

By Kathy Garver
"Cissy"
with Geoffrey Mark

The Family Affair Cookbook
© 2009 Kathy Garver. All Rights Reserved.

All illustrations are copyright of their respective owners, and are also reproduced here in the spirit of publicity. Whilst we have made every effort to acknowledge specific credits whenever possible, we apologize for any omissions, and will undertake every effort to make any appropriate changes in future editions of this book if necessary.

No part of this book may be reproduced in any form or by any means, electronic, mechanical, digital, photocopying or recording, except for the inclusion in a review, without permission in writing from the publisher.

Published in the USA by:
BearManor Media
P O Box 71426
Albany, Georgia 31708
www.bearmanormedia.com

ISBN 1-59393-458-0

Printed in the United States of America.

Book and cover design by Darlene Swanson of Van-garde Imagery, Inc.

The Family Affair Cookbook

An early publicity still for *Family Affair*.

Dedication

This book is dedicated to the memories of some dear friends who are lost and will never be forgotten. Without them, there would have been no Family Affair and you would not be holding this book in your hands. I miss them every day:

Brian Keith
Anissa Jones
Sebastian Cabot
Gregg Fedderson
John Williams
Nancy Walker

This book is also dedicated to my own Family Affair: Mom, Dad, Beverly, Bud and Lance and my other treasured family affair, my husband David and son, Reid. Without their love and consistent support through the years, you would also not be holding this book in your hand. I thank them every day!

The five of us clowning for publicity in 1966.

Contents

Dedication v

Contents vii

About the Author ix

Also by Geoffrey Mark. xxi

Foreword by Dawn Wells xxiii

Introduction xxvii

Recipes from Mr. French's Kitchen 1

Mid-Century Recipes for the Rich and Famous 53

Uncle Bill's Libations and Potent Potables:
Classic Cocktail Recipes from the 1960s 77

Buffy and Jody's Recipes for Children 87

Cissy Sizzles: Kathy's Rousing Recipes 101

Cooking Up a Good Show: They Made It All Possible 149

Index 168

Looking sultry in season three.

About the Author

Most fondly remembered for her starring role as Cissy in the long-running CBS international television hit Family Affair, Kathy Garver has also garnered critical acclaim in movies, radio, voice-over animation, audio book narration and on stage.

Hollywood's legendary Cecil B. DeMille was one of the first to recognize Kathy's distinct talents. Originally hired for a small part in the epic motion picture The Ten Commandments, Kathy was noticed by the great director, who had special scenes written into the movie to highlight the little girl. Kathy's work in The Ten Commandments followed her first film, The Night of the Hunter, directed by Academy Award-winner Charles Laughton.

Garver was born in Long Beach, California, to Hayes and Rosemary Garver, a fourth sibling to her sister Beverly and her brothers Hayes, Jr. and Lance. An extremely intelligent child from a family of ambitious people (Beverly entered UCLA at a precocious fifteen years old), by the time Kathy was a teenager she had added radio and stage credits to her already burgeoning film and television career.

Miss G was a freshman majoring in speech at UCLA when

she was tested for a television series to be called Family Affair. The production was an unusual one – the star of the show, muscular Brian Keith, would only work three months out of the year. All of his scenes in all of the episodes would be shot first, and then the rest of the company would continue working for six more months to finish the approximately thirty-two episodes per season. As the cast would also include six year-old Johnny Whitaker as Jody and almost eight-year-old Anissa Jones as Buffy, the producers were in a quandary. Since the child actors were restricted by law as to how many hours per day they could work, and Keith's time on the set was limited, they needed another actor who could both play a talented teenager yet be old enough to work as many hours needed to get the show filmed on time and on budget.

Sebastian Cabot rounded out the cast perfectly as gentleman's gentleman Mr. French, but he was already a star and did not savor working overtime. The answer to the producer's problems was to find an adult actress who was skilled enough to believably play a fifteen-year-old with a wide range of emotions, intelligent enough to be able to stay in character even if pieces of her scenes were filmed months apart, beautiful enough to be a pin-up girl, and who had such a strong work ethic that she would not mind working well into the evening to do her close-ups after the other actors had left the set (often, Kathy would have to do her close-ups facing a broom, a photo of another cast member, or the cigar-smoking assistant director!). Hundreds of actresses were tested before they found the perfect Cissy in Kathy Garver.

She won accolades, such as Best Actress from the Family Television Awards and the Golden Halo Award and Emerald Award for her lifetime achievement in the entertainment world.

About the Author   xi

Moses and me! My first big break: doing a scene with Charlton Heston in *The Ten Commandments*.

Getting ready to appear on the radio; this is my earliest publicity photo!

About the Author   xiii

On the set of the film *Night of the Hunter* with Charles Laughton (the director) and Lillian Gish. Mr. Laughton shows us how to cut out paper dolls!

After The Night of the Hunter, I continued to work in Film, TV, and Radio. Here I am in an episode of TV's *"This is the Life"*.

xiv   The Family Affair Cookbook

June Lockhart and Kathy in *Death Valley Days*. This telepic helped secure Kathy's part as "Cissy" in *Family Affair* - her role convinced producers she was a great actress and could look and act younger than her years.

CBS publicity shot of Kathy and Sebastian Cabot to promote their TV hosting of the Macy's Thanksgiving Day Parade.

She has a star on the Palm Springs Walk of Fame. Kathy's likeness was found on lunchboxes, comic books, fan magazines, coloring books and even paper dolls. The premier magazine of the industry, legendary TV Guide, featured her several times both on the cover and with feature articles. Her fan mail filled huge sacks every week; such was her popularity around the world.

After the series ended its hugely successful run, Kathy flew to the Middle East to star in an Israeli musical stage version of the show. Learning her lines phonetically, Garver played Cissy in perfect Hebrew! Later, she spent time in London studying at the prestigious Royal Academy of Dramatic Arts, preparing her for starring stage roles in such diverse plays as Romeo and Juliet, My Fair Lady, Sunday in New York, A Midsummer Night's Dream and The Trojan Women. Continuing her studies, Kathy earned a Master's Degree in Theatre Arts from UCLA. She also starred in and produced, with renowned impresario James Doolittle, such immense stage successes as Vanities.

Today, Kathy Garver continues to be a sought-after actress and celebrity. Her recent films include Power and Pride, Technicolor Llama, The Princess Diaries, FBI Murders and Black August. She's a stand-out in the very competitive field of voice-overs for cartoons, commercials and audio books. Garver also produced, narrated and wrote original lyrics and music for eight audio Beatrix Potter tales and eight Mother Goose audios, which have sold over two million copies and won numerous awards. She has won the prestigious Audie Award three times for her work, and has been nominated an astounding seven times. Kathy's voice can be heard on such films as Apollo 13, Ransom, Backdraft and Jingle All the Way, proving she is a favorite of master director Ron Howard.

Miss Garver has electrified the talk-show circuit, entertain-

Kathy dubbed "Hollywood Debutante of the Year" by the Hollywood Chamber of Commerce.

About the Author　　xvii

The height of 1960s sophistication, that's me!

Kathy and Tricia Nixon host a luncheon at the White House for The March of Dimes. Kathy was the National Youth Chairman for this excellent organization

ing audiences of her long career in show business. She's chatted with Bill O'Reilly, Geraldo Rivera, Sally Jessy Raphael, Mary Hart, Maury Povich, and many more about marriage, career, family and the stresses of the modern woman. Her personal appearances at autograph shows, western shows, memorabilia shows, cooking shows, cruises and her own one-woman show keep her constantly busy and in the public eye. Miss G has used her wealth of experience and education to entertain and instruct thousands of people with her exciting and successful motivational and interactive speeches and presentations. From keynote speaker to host to workshop leader, Kathy has enriched the lives of those who have been able to listen and learn from her inspirational communications.

Kathy has her own family affair, which includes her husband David and son Reid. They immensely enjoy sitting at the dinner table, sharing their experiences of the day and munching marvelous meals from the kitchen. Everyone helps in the Garver/Travis household, from setting the table to stirring the soup to clearing and washing the dishes. Kathy's married family has greatly helped in honing the fabulous recipes you are soon to enjoy!

The Family poses in season three. That is Brian's head pasted on a stand-in's body!

Also by Geoffrey Mark

First Lady of Song: Ella Fitzgerald for the Record

The Lucy Book

Ethel Merman: The Biggest Star on Broadway

First season photo shoot in 1966.

Foreword by Dawn Wells

It is inevitable. Oh, not the connection with Gilligan's Island or even being referred to as Mary Ann. I got used to that years ago and am proud of my association with such a television icon. Despite the literally dozens of plays I have done on the stage and all of the film, television and radio work I have done over a career that has lasted longer than I care to tell you, it is inevitable.

It is inevitable that no matter where I go, some nice fan will ask me for my recipe for coconut cream pie! And I have thirteen recipes!

Why is this? Perhaps because it seems that Mary Ann was able to bake one in a matter of minutes with almost no ingredients and no oven whatsoever. Or maybe it is because I myself am the author of The Mary Ann Gilligan's Island Cookbook with three generations of family recipes. And, of course, Mary Ann - she did the laundry, grew radioactive vegetables, restyled the Castaway's wardrobe, swept the huts and was the sole cook on the island making 1,000 recipes out of coconuts and bananas – now that I think of it, did any other woman actually work on that island?

I am so pleased Kathy Garver has written this book. Despite being friends for many years, she and I have very different viewpoints on many things. Kathy is a wife and mother, actress, producer, author, teacher, and sought-after voice over talent. I have been single much of my life, took care of an ex-husband with leukemia and my mother until she was 94, was not fortunate enough to have any children and am a serious working actress, producer, journalist and motivational speaker. We share a passion for our work and for creating in the kitchen. Everyone who loves Kathy has been begging her to do this for years. Some wanted her to do an autobiography, others a tome about Family Affair and still others a great cookbook featuring her wonderful cooking. Between these pages, I think Miss G has managed to make all of us happy. I have also known Geoffrey Mark for several years; he is a walking encyclopedia of pop culture, a great writer and quite a cook himself!

What you won't find here are sordid details about her personal life or the making of the show. First of all, I don't think Kathy has any sordid details – she has been too busy working and raising a family to be sordid. Secondly, she is very loving and respectful of the people who made up that wonderful show, Family Affair, and wouldn't hurt them by sharing things that are no one's business. Kathy tells us what we need to know in a most enjoyable way and then concentrates on the food.

I love how things are arranged here, and cannot wait to try all of the enjoyable, retro-recipes laid out for us. They are easy to follow, fun to make and just delicious! Listen, if you can't trust a woman who can bake a coconut cream pie from scratch with almost no ingredients and no oven, who can you trust?

Dawn Wells
June 2009

Day of the installation of my "Star" – 1995!

Love the eyelashes! This photo was used to grace the cover of three magazines!

Introduction

Family Affair was one of the warmest and most enduring television series of the 1960s and 1970s. A top-ten rated show, its popularity further soared as a hit in syndication. A fortune was made for the owners of the show, with more gold added to the coffers when the series was recently released on DVD. Excellent bonus features for each of the seasons enrich the experience of watching the beloved series. The individual seasons were the best-selling sets ever for the distributor, MPI, prompting them to release a large box-set of the entire series a year ahead of schedule. The appeal of *Family Affair* is enduring, attracting and charming affluent baby-boomers who remember the show with affection as well as youngsters who are discovering the show for the first time. I should know; I was one of the stars of the show and meet literally thousands of fans every year as I travel the world.

The hallmark of the series was its attitude. Unlike many of the "family" sitcoms that preceded it, *Family Affair* did not tie up all the answers to the family's problems in a neat little package by the end of each episode: people died, children got sick and did not get better, friendships ended, and poor people stayed poor. In fact, the entire series had a touch of melancholy to it because of its origin story. A couple dies in an accident, leaving fifteen-year-old Cissy (that's me!) and six-year-old fraternal twins Buffy and Jody orphaned. Internationally famous architect, builder and millionaire Bill Davis receives these children (his nieces and nephew), literally dropped off on his doorstep by selfish relatives who want to get rid of them. However, with the help of his reluctant gentleman's gentleman Giles French, a new family is born.

Certainly, *Family Affair* was not the first series to bring their characters together from tragedy. In fact, the list of parents who had to die for sitcoms to be born is almost ghoulish: *Bachelor Father*, *My Three Sons*, *The Danny Thomas Show*, *The Andy Griffith Show*, *The Lucy Show*, *The Doris Day Show*, *Julia*, *The Brady Bunch*, *The Partridge Family*, *Who's the Boss?*, *The Nanny* – sitcom history is filled with off-screen funerals. But with one exception, these losses are almost never referred to and are forgotten after the initial episodes establish the premise.

Not so with *Family Affair*. These children never forget their parents no matter how much time passes, and are always aware that tragedy may come just around the next corner. The show's scripts, supervised by legendary Austin and Irma Kalish, may sometimes be simple but never simple-minded. Character development was never trampled on just for the sake of jokes, and the heart of the show was the love these people had for one another.

Nowhere is that affection more apparent than the scenes when the family all gathers around the table to share a meal. Now your family can share their love around your table with the same recipes the Davis family enjoyed.

Think of your own childhoods. Aren't there certain memories tied to food – a certain dish your mother or grandmother prepared that was a favorite, perhaps the smell of chicken soup simmering on a Friday evening or bacon sizzling on a Sunday morning or those potatoes that Aunt Lenore always served on Thanksgiving? For me, there are times I can inhale food cooking, close my eyes and be instantly transported to a place and time that no longer exists, with loved ones that are now gone.

At the Davis dinner table, the bachelor uncle re-learned first grade math and got an earful about what was hip in the teenage circles. Mr. French made the most of meals, yet grumbled that his Escargot was not thoroughly appreciated. Jody thought snails definitely belonged in the garden and Buffy wanted to take them to show and tell. Cissy thought they were fattening and Uncle Bill silently thought he'd rather eat them at a quiet French restaurant with his current amour.

Cissy's culinary sense was awakened when she walked by the kitchen in an episode, nose in the air, sniffing and saying, "Chicken Marengo, Mr. French?"

Bill Davis and Giles French smugly believed they were doing pretty well in "this parenting thing," but Mr. French winced at the fact that, "She's growing up, isn't she, sir?"

One of the reasons I wrote this book was to help evoke those happy memories for our fans, as well as to encourage you to make new, 21st-century memories for your families. This cookbook is not just steeped in nostalgia; there are recipes and lessons to be applied to today's families as well. Whether you live by yourself and want to throw a party for your pals, are working parents with time constraints or want to start new family traditions, there is something here for most everyone.

I have screened all of the episodes of *Family Affair* to remember exactly what it was we in the Davis family ate back in the day.

Our palates certainly were secure with the skills of Mr. French! Along the way, wonderful memories rushed back of working with Brian Keith, Sebastian Cabot, Anissa Jones, Johnny Whitaker and our wonderful guest stars. Whenever a recipe sparked one of those recollections, I wrote it down to share with you in the following pages.

As long as I was taking a walk back through the cuisine of the 1960s, I decided to include the classic gourmet recipes of the era, many of which have surprisingly fallen out of fashion. For many, I have included a 21st-century upgrade to make the recipes applicable to today's living.

Have you been to a bar or club lately? Alcoholic drinks have become elegant again, just as they were in Uncle Bill's day. Gathered in this book are classic drinks of that era, so you can astound your friends with elegance and creativity! So we don't leave out the children, there is a chapter on the foods I remember that Buffy and Jody (and Anissa and Johnny) really enjoyed, with recipes that the children in your life will not only love but can help prepare. Finally, I wanted to share a nice dollop of Kathy Garver, so I have included recipes that have been favorites in my family for years.

You may notice that sometimes I will share a thought with you as Kathy, and sometimes you will hear from Cissy. I am not leading two lives, I just wanted to have some fun and share that fun with you!

I trust this book will make your kitchen glow with joy, fun and good eating. Try the recipes, enjoy the recollections and may your table be surrounded by the delight of a *Family Affair*!
Love,
Kathy
www.kathygarver.com

One of my favorite publicity photos, from season five.

Talented and handsome, Sebastian Cabot was
a joy and a pleasure to work with!

Recipes from
Mr. French's Kitchen

Uncle Bill's Favorite Breakfast: Eggs Benedict

Episode Two: Jody and Cissy

Although Anissa had the first episode pretty much to herself, the second episode is the one that rounded out and deepened the family with Buffy's brother and sister, Cissy and Jody. When I watch the show today, I am not only moved by the poignancy and the subtlety of the writing and acting, but I am appalled at the wig I was wearing for this outing as Cissy, the same one I wore in all of the pre-production photographs that were taken. I loathed wearing that awful thing and, believe me, it was the last time!

    On to cooking! Eggs Benedict is the first dish mentioned in the series that Mr. French prepares. It basically consists of half a buttered English muffin at the bottom, which is topped firstly with Canadian-style bacon, otherwise known as back bacon, followed by a perfectly poached egg and lastly, drizzled with

A candid photo of Uncle Bill, Mr. French and Cissy
taken on the set of Family Affair.

smooth Hollandaise sauce. For a heavier meal, Eggs Benedict is often served with roasted potatoes or homemade fries, which are used to mop up the gloriously yummy, runny egg yolk. To prepare this delectable dish, you may find yourself having to contend with several things at once, as most of the ingredients only take a few minutes to prepare. It will take quite a bit of skill and expertise, but with a little practice or an extra pair of hands, you will soon be making Eggs Benedict like a true professional.

To start, it is best to prepare the Hollandaise sauce, as this can easily be reheated and stirred quickly when needed (although if not served immediately, one has to be prepared for a few lumps). Next, the eggs can be poached for a few minutes in simmering water. While the eggs are cooking, the bacon can be grilled or fried for a few minutes. While all this is going on, use your other four arms to split and toast the English muffins.

Ingredients:
4 fresh English muffins
8 rashers of back bacon
8 eggs
1 tsp of white vinegar
4 egg yolks
2 tbsp of lemon juice
9 oz. of butter
pinch of cayenne pepper
salt and pepper to taste

To make a simple Hollandaise sauce, place the 4 egg yolks, lemon juice, cayenne pepper and the salt and pepper into a fairly large saucepan and with a hand whisk, whisking all the ingredients until they have blended together. Cut the butter into small chunks and add to the saucepan. Turn the heat on the burner to medium and begin to whisk the ingredients. As the butter melts, make sure that you blend it thoroughly into the egg yolks. Continue to whisk vigorously until all of the butter has blended into the eggs. If the sauce begins to separate, add 2 tsp of water to the sauce mixture and whisk briskly until the mixture has combined together to form a creamy sauce. Once all of the butter has melted and a sauce has been formed, continue whisking until the sauce thickens to the desired consistency. Add more salt and pepper if required. Remove from the heat and keep the sauce warm before serving for up to 30 minutes.

Once the Hollandaise sauce has been prepared and set to one side, you can concentrate on the other ingredients. The next step is to prepare the eggs and the bacon, if possible simultaneously. Preheat the frying pan to a moderate heat and cut the bacon into circles that will just cover the base of the muffin. At the same time, start to poach the eggs. Place the bacon on the frying pan and cook on both sides until browned. Keep warm if the eggs are still cooking.

When the eggs and the bacon are almost ready, cut the muffins in half lengthwise evenly and place them in the toaster. When the muffins have been lightly toasted, butter them generously and place in the middle of a warmed plate. Remove the bacon from the pan and sit one circular piece on top of each half muffin. Arrange the drained and trimmed poached egg on top of the bacon or ham and finally spoon the warmed Hollandaise sauce over the egg. Serve immediately. Certainly, you can use an egg poacher to simplify the recipe, and I will not tell anyone if you choose to use a Hollandaise sauce mix (Knorr makes an excellent one).

It seems that many people all over the world love the Eggs Benedict recipe and have enjoyed adapting it to their tastes and local ingredients to create plenty of new recipes for everyone to try. Read the following variations to see whether there are any that you would like to create in your kitchen:

Eggs Florentine - replace the bacon with spinach.

Eggs Maryland - delete the bacon and English muffin and serve poached eggs drizzled with Hollandaise sauce on top of crab cakes.

Waldorf Style Eggs - replace the English muffin with toast and serve with poached eggs, sautéed mushrooms and mushroom sauce.

Norwegian Eggs - replace the bacon with thin slices of smoked salmon or lox.

Artichoke Eggs - replace the English muffin with cooked artichoke hearts.

Eggs Blackstone - use streaky bacon instead of back bacon and add a slice of tomato.

Country Eggs Benedict - Replace the bacon with sausage slices and cover with sausage gravy instead of Hollandaise sauce.

Mr. French's Family Yorkshire Pudding
Episode Five: Marmalade

When Mr. French's grandmother used to make Yorkshire pudding to go with the Sunday roast, they would eat it the true Yorkshire way. That is, as a first course with just savory gravy poured over it. After all, the original idea of Yorkshire pudding was to fill you up so that you don't want so much more of the expensive meat! If there were any of the Pudding left over as a treat we Davis kids would have it as a dessert with Golden Syrup poured over it.

Ingredients:
1 cup plain flour
1 cup egg
1 cup milk
1 tsp extra virgin olive oil
Salt

Preheat the oven to 425°. Put a tsp of oil in each of several muffin tins or, to be truly Yorkshire, a couple of tbl in a larger roasting tin and place in the oven until the oil is really hot and beginning to smoke. Meanwhile, combine the rest of the ingredients and beat to form a batter of the consistency of double cream. If you wish, you can add mixed dried herbs to add a savory flavor. When the oil is smoking, take the tin out of the oven and place it over a low flame so that it doesn't cool as you add the batter. Pour in the batter; if you're using muffin tins don't over-fill. Remember that the puddings will rise and puff up. Put the tin back into the top of the oven as soon as possible and leave for about 20-25 minutes, by which time they will be puffed up and crisp.

Bouillabaisse a la Marseillaise

Episode Five: Marmalade

How to make the authentic bouillabaisse is always a point of contention among cooking experts; each always insists that his (or her) own is the only correct version. If you do not happen to live on the Mediterranean, you cannot obtain the particular rockfish, gurnards, mullets, weavers, sea eels, wrasses, and breams which they consider the absolutely essential fish for bouillabaisse. You can still make an extremely good facsimile even if you have only frozen fish and canned clam juice to work with, because all the other essential flavors of tomatoes, onion or leeks, garlic, herbs, and olive oil are easily available.

Bouillabaisse is really fish chowder; whole small fish or large fish cut into serving pieces are boiled in a deliciously aromatic fish broth. The fish are served on a platter, and the broth in a tureen, and you eat both together in large soup plates.

For the best and most interesting flavor, pick six or more

varieties of fish, which is why a bouillabaisse is ideally made for at least six people. Some of the fish should be firm fleshed and gelatinous, like halibut or eel; some should be tender and flaky like whiting and sole. The firm fish hold their shape, and the tender fish partially fall apart in the soup. Shellfish, like clams and mussels, are optional, but always add glamour and color if you wish to include them.

Except for live lobsters and crabs, all the fish may be cleaned, sliced, and refrigerated several hours before the final cooking. The soup base may be boiled, strained, and refrigerated ahead of time. The actual cooking of the fish in the soup will take only about 20 minutes, and then the dish should be served immediately.

Fish for bouillabaisse should be lean, and have the best and freshest-smelling quality. Here are some suggestions: bass, cod, sea eel, flounder, grouper, haddock, whiting, halibut, perch, pollock, snapper, sea trout, crab, lobster, mussels, clams, scallops. Have the fish cleaned and scaled; discard gills. Save heads, bones, and trimmings for the soup base. Cut large fish into crosswise slices two inches wide. Scrub clams; scrub and soak mussels; wash scallops. If using live crab or lobster split just before cooking; remove sand sack and intestinal tube from lobsters, and tail flap from under crabs.

Ingredients for soup base:
1 cup sliced yellow onions
¾ to 1 cup sliced leeks, white part only; or ½ cup more onions
½ cup of extra virgin olive oil
2 to 3 cups chopped fresh tomatoes, or 1¼ cups drained
    canned tomatoes, or ¼ cup tomato paste
4 cloves mashed garlic
2½ quarts water

6 parsley sprigs
1 bay leaf
½ tsp thyme or basil
1/8 tsp fennel
2 big pinches of saffron
A 2-inch piece or ½ tsp dried orange peel
1/8 tsp pepper
1 tbl salt (none if using clam juice)
3 to 4 lbs. fish heads, bones, and trimmings, including shellfish remains; or, 1 quart clam juice and 1½ quarts of water, and no salt

Cook the onions and leeks slowly in the olive oil for 5 minutes without browning. Stir in the tomatoes and garlic, and cook 5 minutes more. Add the water, herbs, seasoning, and fish or clam juice to the kettle. Bring to a boil, skim, and cook, uncovered, at a slow boil for 30 to 40 minutes. Strain the soup and correct the seasoning, if necessary. Set aside, uncovered, until cool. If you are not finishing the bouillabaisse immediately, then refrigerate.

Cooking the Bouillabaisse:

Bring the soup base to a rapid boil in the kettle about 20 minutes before serving. Add lobsters, crabs, and firm-fleshed fish. Bring quickly back to the boil and boil rapidly, uncovered, for 5 minutes. Then add the tender-fleshed fish, and the clams, mussels, and scallops. Bring back to a boil again for 5 minutes. Do not overcook.

Immediately lift out the fish and arrange on the platter. Carefully taste soup for seasoning, place 6 to 8 slices of bread in the tureen, and pour in the soup. Spoon a ladleful of soup over the fish, and sprinkle parsley over both fish and soup. Serve immediately.

Orange Marmalade

Episode Five: Marmalade

Sebastian Cabot was at his acting best in this episode. His comedy timing is right on the money, as is his expression when he finally tastes the terrible commercial marmalade he was hired to endorse in a TV show. Being a proper Englishman (actually, Sebastian Cabot was raised in Canada – see how good an actor he was?), Mr. French knew exactly how to make a proper orange marmalade; here is his recipe!

Ingredients:
2 lbs oranges
2 large lemons
8 cups water
8 cups sugar

Wash oranges and lemons, removing stem parts but leaving fruits whole. Place whole fruits in a large enamel kettle; cover with water. Cover and bring to a boil; simmer until a fork will pierce fruit easily, about 1½ hours. Remove fruit to cool completely; set kettle with liquid aside.

When fruits are cooled, cut in half lengthwise. Cut the fruit into thin slices using a very sharp knife. Remove seeds and reserve. Return seeds to juice in kettle and boil 10 minutes. Strain juice and return to kettle. Add fruit slices to kettle and bring to a boil. Add sugar, stirring until dissolved, and continue boiling (stirring just to prevent scorching) until juices start to thicken and temperature reaches about 221F° at sea level or to 9° above your boiling point.

Remove from heat and skim off foam. Pour immediately into hot sterilized ½ pint jars, leaving ½-inch headspace. Place seals on and adjust rings. Process jars in boiling water bath for 5 minutes or follow manufacturer's directions for your altitude. Adjust lids again if necessary and cool upright.

Chicken Chow Mein

Episode Six: Room with a Viewpoint

Uncle Bill is often seen out on the town, squiring some beautiful lady to dinner in little old New York. This was done partially to remind the audience what a swinging stud Uncle Bill had been before the children arrived, and partially to give Brian Keith scenes he could film independently of the rest of the cast. In some cases, these restaurant scenes are the only footage of Brian in an episode! In this episode, Bill goes to an elegant Chinese restaurant. In those days, the menus at Chinese restaurants were much more limited than they are today. In New York City, many such restaurants had neon signs that simply said "Chow Mein." This dish was the heart of these restaurants, and Mr. French had his own recipe to serve us at home.

Ingredients:
1 lb chicken meat
1 cup celery, chopped
1 lb bok choy
½ lb fresh mushrooms, sliced
½ lb dry wonton noodles
2 tbls extra virgin olive oil
1 lb bean sprouts or snow pea pods
1 medium onion, sliced

1 green onion, diced along the diagonal
1 carrot, sliced
1 red pepper, sliced

Seasonings for Chicken:
1 tsp soy sauce
1 to 2 tsp oyster sauce
salt and pepper to taste
less than 1 tsp of cornstarch

Gravy:
1 tbl cornstarch
1 tbl oyster sauce
1 tsp soy sauce
½ cup water
salt or accent, if desired, and pepper to taste

Wash the bean sprouts and give them time to drain. Boil noodles in salted boiling water until they are soft, but not sticky. Break the noodles in half, if desired, so they are easier to manage. Blanch the noodles in cold water and drain. Cut the chicken into thin strips. Add seasoning ingredients to chicken, adding cornstarch last.

Marinate chicken in seasonings for 10 to 15 minutes. While chicken is marinating, prepare vegetables. Cut the bok choy diagonally into ½-inch-thick slices, slice mushrooms. Heat the frying pan on high, add 2 tbls of oil and fry the noodles in small portions until they are golden. Use chopsticks to separate the noodles as they are frying. Remove the noodles. Add more oil and add the meat and onion to the pan. Stir-fry until the meat has no redness. Remove from wok or pan.

Cook the rest of the vegetables separately, adding a bit of salt, if desired, to taste. With the bean sprouts and bok choy add a bit of sugar as well, if desired. If desired, add about ¼ cup of water and cover pan while cooking bok choy, as it doesn't contain much moisture. Give the gravy a quick stir. Add all the ingredients back into the wok, making a well in the middle of the wok for the gravy. Mix well. Add green onions at this point, if desired, or save them for a garnish. Pour on top of the noodles. Garnish with sesame seeds.

Lebanese Stuffed Grape Leaves

Episode Eight: Who's Afraid of Nural Shperri?

This is one of the rare times Mr. French was shown having any sort of a love interest. A Lebanese family tried to manipulate Mr. French into marrying their over-aged daughter. Sebastian had a field day with this one! Between you and me, I was always rooting for Miss Favisham as a love interest. Didn't you think that she and Giles had a little something going on his days off? I thought Heather Angel was a beautiful actress – lovely and in control. She had Mr. French right where she wanted him! Although I did not know her acting background, I could sense that she was quite accomplished and I watched diligently the way she portrayed her "nanny" role with graceful aplomb. I later learned that she was quite a distinguished English actress, having appeared in *The Hound of the Baskervilles, Pride and Prejudice* and even in Alfred Hitchcock's *Lifeboat*. She created a role in the *Bulldog Drummond* series and played in five films of that name. She attained a star on the Walk of Fame in Hollywood – Brian Keith was awarded that honor posthumously in June of 2008. She certainly added a wonderful touch of class to

Recipes from Mr. French's Kitchen 13

The nannies and Mr. French plus...Mrs. Beasley.

our show and I'm sure, on Mr. French's day off, she even taught him a thing or two about gourmet cooking!

I often thought it would have been a good idea for Mr. French and Miss Favisham to get together; it would have been nice to have a woman in the house to share things with teen-aged Cissy! Also in the cast that week were future Alice star Vic Tayback and Henry Corden (who was the second man to voice Fred Flintstone after Alan Reed's death).

This recipe is very versatile, because these grape leaves can be served hot, cold, as a side dish, in a salad or even on a sandwich!

Ingredients:
Grape leaves
Ground lamb
Rice
Salt and Pepper
Cinnamon
tomato paste

Mix the lamb and raw rice in a ratio of 2 (meat) to 1 (rice). Season with salt, pepper and cinnamon and don't be afraid of the cinnamon. Optional additions are a generous handful of fresh minced parsley and/or a chopped tomato. Rinse the grape leaves. Remove the largest part of the center vein. Many of the leaves that come in jars are large enough to cut in half. Find the way that is best for you. Put about 1 tsp of mixture onto each leaf and roll like a burrito, wrapping up the sides and turning up the bottom until it resembles a little cigarette. Tuck each one neatly into a heavy pot. Place them close together so they won't fall apart. The yield should be about fifty. Make a thin sauce by stirring a spoonful of tomato paste into some warm water. Cover the stuffed grape leaves with this thin sauce. Place a saucer on top of the leaves so they won't float. Simmer for 30 minutes or so until the leaves are tender and the rice is cooked. Serve hot or cold.

Hearts of Palm Salad

Episode Nine: A Matter for Experts

This dish was popular because it was considered delicate in nature for the genteel folks who ate it. Actually, it is quite nutritious and a fine light luncheon, first course or snack.

Ingredients:

2 tbls lemon juice
(1) 14 oz. can of hearts of palm, drained and sliced
2 tbls finely-chopped stuffed green olives
½ tsp aromatic bitters
1 tsp sugar
1/3 cup extra virgin olive oil
1 tsp finely-chopped celery
1 tsp finely-chopped onion
¼ tsp paprika
½ tsp salt
6 cups torn Bibb or Butter lettuce

Combine salad oil, lemon juice, sugar, salt, bitters, paprika, olives, onion and celery; beat well. Chill. At serving time, toss together hearts of palm and lettuce in salad bowl. Add dressing and toss.

Creamed Cauliflower and Peas

Episode Nine: A Matter for Experts

We were often shown at the dinner table eating non-descript meals. Sometimes, the prop people didn't even give us real food – we just pushed ersatz imposters around in our plates while we said our lines. I was watching this episode recently and noticed this dish, which was real because I remember eating it and enjoying it. I am sure you will, too!

Ingredients:
1 large cauliflower – separated into florets
Salt
1 package frozen peas
Milk
½ cup cracker crumbs
¼ tbl nutmeg
¼ tbl white pepper
1 cup light cream
3 tbls flour
¾ cup finely-chopped onion
¼ cup plus 2 tbls butter

Cook cauliflower in 1½ cups water and salt; bring to boiling. Reduce heat and simmer covered 10 to 15 minutes. Drain. Cook peas in ¼ cup water and salt; bring to boiling. Reduce heat and simmer covered for 5 minutes. Drain peas and reserve liquid. Add enough milk to make 2 cups. Set aside. In ¼ cup hot butter, sauté onion until golden. Remove from heat and stir in flour, salt, pepper and nutmeg. Stir in reserved liquid and cream; return to heat, bring to boiling, stirring constantly. Gently combine peas, cauliflower and sauce in casserole. Combine cracker crumbs and melted butter, sprinkle over casserole. Bake covered 30 minutes and uncovered 30 minutes at 350°.

Crepes Suzette

Episode Eleven: Take Two Aspirins

Once considered haute cuisine, this French version of pancakes is rarely served in restaurants anymore. Be very careful when trying to flambé!

Ingredients:

1 cup sifted all-purpose flour
¼ tsp salt
2 tbls sugar
½ tsp ground cinnamon
1 cup milk
2 tbls melted butter
2 eggs, slightly beaten
1 cup orange marmalade or apricot jam
Powdered sugar
2 tbls butter
1 tbl cognac or Cointreau, optional

Put milk, melted butter and eggs in blender container or food processor bowl. Combine flour, salt, sugar and cinnamon. Add to milk mixture; blend until smooth. Allow batter to sit at room temperature about 10-15 minutes.

Heat a 5-inch skillet or crepe pan and grease lightly. Pour in about 3 tbls of batter; swirl around until batter covers bottom. Cook until crepe is brown on the bottom; turn and brown other side. Keep crepes warm in a 200° oven until all crepes are cooked.

When all ready, place 2 tbls marmalade or jam in center of each crepe. Roll; dust with powdered sugar. Heat butter in a chafing dish with remaining ½ cup jam or marmalade and the cognac or liqueur. Place rolled up crepes in the chafing dish. Spoon hot sauce over the crepes for 1 or 2 minutes, while sauce bubbles around them. Serve on warmed dessert plates.

To flambé: fill a large serving spoon with cognac. Ignite it with a match. Stir into remaining sauce in chafing dish. Quickly spoon the sauce, while still flaming, over the rolled crepes. Any heatproof shallow casserole type dish can be used in place of a chafing dish. This recipe is Classic, from the time when chafing dishes were very popular.

Antipasto

Episode Thirteen: Love Me, Love Me Not

It is hard to remember a time when Italian food was considered exotic food in this country. However, most Americans had never tasted pizza until after World War II, when pizza parlors and Italian restaurants began springing up in large cities. The term antipasto refers to the course that is served after the pasta course, which in a traditional Italian meal is served first. This combination of salad ingredients and cold cuts was supposed to clear the palate for the meat, fish or chicken dish to follow.

Ingredients:
Italian Salami
Smoked provolone cheese
Green olives stuffed with feta cheese
Celery hearts
Artichoke hearts, marinated
Hearts of Palm
Roasted red peppers
Garbanzo beans
Anchovy fillets, drained
Pickled beets
Bibb lettuce
Green onions
Roma tomato wedges
Extra Virgin olive oil
Balsamic vinegar
Pepper
Salt
Oregano
½ cup grated Romano cheese

Arrange lettuce on a lovely, large platter. Add the rest of the ingredients in bunches on the lettuce individually. Drizzle the ingredients with oil and vinegar and add salt, pepper, oregano and Romano cheese to taste.

Charlotte Russe

Episode Seventeen: All Around the House
This dessert was once known as both a fancy society dessert and a namesake treat enjoyed by children on the streets of New

York City. Both versions are essentially the same, except the one for kids came in a paper wrapper which one pushed up from the bottom to get to the goodies. Buffy and Jody would pester Mr. French into either making it with dinner or stopping on the way home from school to get a store-made snack. Presented here is the version for adults.

Ingredients for the sponge cake:
4 large eggs
1 cup sugar
4 tbls cold water
1 tsp vanilla extract
1 tsp lemon extract
1 cups all-purpose flour
1 tsp baking powder
½ tsp salt

Ingredients for the whipped cream and decoration:
1 cup heavy cream, well chilled
2 tsp powdered sugar
½ tsp vanilla
Maraschino cherries
Chocolate sprinkles

Preheat oven to 350°. Butter and flour a 9-inch-by-13-inch cake pan. Chill bowl and beaters for whipping cream. In a mixer bowl, beat the eggs and sugar together with an electric mixer until the mixture is smooth and lemon yellow in color. Mix in the cold water, vanilla extract and lemon extract. Sift together the flour, baking powder and salt. Fold into the egg mixture. Stir by hand until flour is just incorporated, don't over mix

Pour the batter into the prepared pan. Smooth the top with a spatula. Bake for 35 to 45 minutes, until a toothpick inserted in the center comes out clean. Cool on a rack.

In the chilled bowl, beat the cream on medium or medium high speed until it begins to thicken. Mix in the vanilla and, about ½ tsp at a time, the powdered sugar. Beat cream just until it forms stiff peaks. Refrigerate until ready to use. Cut sponge cake rounds with a 3-inch cookie cutter. Unless you can find food-grade cardboard tubes, you're probably going to have to plop or pipe the whipped cream on the sponge cake rounds. If really necessary, throw on some chocolate sprinkles, but always top each serving with a Maraschino cherry.

Suggestions: Cut off a very thin slice of the baked top - the whipped cream sticks to the cake better. Piping is prettier than plopping, but not at all necessary. Before plopping on the whipped cream, try spreading on a thin layer of raspberry or strawberry preserves. Instead of cutting rounds, just cut the cake into squares - no waste.

Untidy Samuel Sandwiches

Episode Twenty: A Helping Hand
This is a very, very old family recipe handed down from Great-Great-Grandmother French. Today, you'd call it Sloppy Joes. It was Buffy and Jody's favorite meal.

Ingredients:
1 lb ground beef
1 medium onion, chopped
¼ cup green pepper, chopped
3 stalks celery, chopped

3/4 cup ketchup
3 tbls vinegar
3 tbls, sugar
1½ tbls mustard
½ tbls Worcestershire sauce
¼ oz. salt pork, finely diced
Salt and pepper - to taste

Brown ground beef, salt pork and onions in a skillet. Drain. Add all remaining ingredients and mix together. Simmer for 30-40 minutes, stirring occasionally. Serve hot on a hamburger roll.

Barquette aux Marrons

Episode Twenty: A Helping Hand

This delicious dessert features boat-shaped pastries filled first with an almond frangipane cream, then a mound of chestnut butter cream and topped with a thin white icing. This extremely fancy dessert is time consuming to make, but well worth the effort. I guarantee your guests will be impressed, which is why Mr. French always went to the trouble of serving it to Uncle Bill's clients!

Ingredients:
9 oz. short crust pastry
For the almond layer:
2½ oz. butter, at room temperature
2½ oz. ground almonds
2½ oz. sugar
1 tsp plain flour
1 egg

1 tsp rum

For the chestnut layer:
9 oz. sweet chestnut puree
2½ oz. unsalted butter, at room temperature
2 tsp rum

For the icing:
1 cup pure icing sugar, sieved
1 tsp melted butter
2 tbl hot water

Preheat oven to 400°. Line Barquette molds with thinly-rolled pastry.

    For the almond layer: Briefly combine the ingredients for the almond layer in a food processor. Spoon into the pastry-lined molds, filling each two-thirds full. Bake for about 12-15 minutes. The almond layer will feel a little springy and will be golden brown. Cool completely.

    For the chestnut layer: Mix ingredients and process for a minute or so until the mixture is very well combined. Divide the chestnut mix between the tartlets, molding each one with a spatula to the traditional domed shape. Place in the refrigerator until the chestnut filling is very firm.

    For the icing: Mix the icing until thick but still pourable and spoon over the cold tartlets.

Curried Chicken and Rice
(Uncle Bill's Favorite Dinner)

Episode Twenty: A Helping Hand

It was a great thrill to be able to work with some of the wonderful actors we had as guest stars on Family Affair. These legends chose to work with us because we were a hit show with excellent scripts, and because of their affection for Brian Keith, Sebastian Cabot or John Williams. In this case, we were overjoyed to have Myrna Loy with us. Miss Loy had been a star since the early 1930s, and her celebrity never wavered. Whether she was doing one of her famous Thin Man films with William Powell, playing the wife in The Best Years of Our Lives or driving Cary Grant crazy in Mr. Blandings Builds His Dream House, Myrna Loy was never anything but excellent in the 129 motion pictures she made. Miss Loy and John Williams had previously worked together in the Doris Day thriller Midnight Lace in 1960.

Already sixty years old when she came to us, Miss Loy was still beautiful, glamorous and ever the feminine lady. I was surprised that she seemed very tentative before the camera, sometimes unsure of her lines and movements. Perhaps the part of a clumsy maid was not right for her elegant image. I recently asked our script consultant Rocky Kalish about it. His answer was very revealing to me as an actress: Miss Loy was wonderful playing straight to comedy actors (William Powell and Cary Grant, to name just two) and reacting to their antics, but needed more than the limited rehearsal time we had in order to play comedy

Recipes from Mr. French's Kitchen   25

Sebastian Cabot and I made the covers of many magazines together!

well herself. Nevertheless, it was a privilege and a joy to be able to act with her, and she continued working for another twenty years as both an actress and activist before she retired.

Ingredients:

1 cup jasmine rice
2 boneless, skinless chicken breasts or thighs (8 oz. each)
1 tbl Chinese rice wine or dry sherry
¼ tsp salt
Pepper
1 tsp corn or potato starch
2 cloves garlic
1 potato
1 yellow onion
1 green onion
3 tbls extra virgin olive oil
4 tbls curry powder
½ cup chicken broth
1 tsp granulated sugar
Salt and pepper to taste

Begin cooking the rice. Cut the chicken into chunks about 1½-to 2-inch square. Add the rice wine, salt, pepper and cornstarch. Marinate the chicken for 25 minutes. While the chicken is marinating, prepare the vegetables. Peel and mince the garlic. Peel the potato and onion. Cut into chunks about same size as the chicken. Cut the green onion on the diagonal into 3-4 pieces. Heat the wok over medium-high to high heat. Add the oil. When the oil is hot, add the onion. Stir-fry until softened. Push up to the side of the wok. Add the curry powder. Stir-fry for about 1½ minutes, and then add the garlic and green onion.

Stir-fry briefly (less than 30 seconds), until the garlic is aromatic and the curry powder flavor is strong. Add the chicken cubes and the potato. Stir-fry until the chicken is nicely coated with the curry and nearly cooked through. Add the chicken broth and sugar. Season with salt and pepper to taste. Reduce the heat to low and simmer, covered, for 15 minutes. Make sure the chicken is cooked through. Add the cornstarch, bring the sauce to a boil, and stir to thicken. Taste and adjust seasonings as required. Serve hot over rice.

Roast Leg of Lamb

Episode Twenty-Seven: The Prize

This was Sebastian Cabot's first aired show after his hand surgery. Many people through the years have asked me about Sebastian's temporary disappearance from our show. There were rumors for years that he'd had a heart attack or another serious illness. If that had been the case, he would have been permanently replaced. The truth of the matter is that our Mr. French needed emergency surgery on his hand. This happened very early in the shooting of our first season, and John Williams was brought in as a short-term replacement. The doctors informed the producers how much time Mr. Cabot would be unable to work, and the writers rewrote already written scripts to accommodate the situation. This was a huge fly in the ointment, because we were filming all of the episodes out of order to placate Brian Keith's working schedule. Only by having all of the episodes already written before we started, and having a crack production team, could we have so seamlessly solved the problem of the revolving Mr. Frenches!

If you watch the episodes in order, there are some episodes

where Mr. French has his hand bandaged, and then he goes away for several weeks to be replaced by John Williams. The episodes where his hand is bandaged were all filmed after he came back, but shown out of shooting order. The reason for this was to establish Sebastian in his character of Mr. French before replacing him, so that the audience (especially the children watching) would not be confused. And to further end more confusion, it was Mr. Cabot as Giles French and Mr. Williams as his brother Nigel French, not Niles as is erroneously stated in several books!

Ingredients:

1/3 cup Dijon-style mustard

1 large garlic clove, minced and mashed to a paste with ¼ tsp salt

1 tbl finely-chopped fresh rosemary leaves or 1 tsp crumbled dried plus fresh rosemary sprigs for garnish

1 tbl finely-chopped fresh thyme leaves or 1 tsp crumbled dried plus fresh thyme sprigs for garnish

1½ tbl soy sauce

¼ cup dry white wine

4 tbl extra virgin olive oil

An 8-lb leg of lamb, the pelvic bone removed and the lamb tied

2 lbs (about 40) small white onions, blanched in boiling water for 2 minutes, drained, and peeled

2 large carrots cut into ½-inch pieces

2½ lbs (about 40) small red or white potatoes, cooked in boiling salted water for 10 minutes, drained, and halved

For the gravy:

Recipes from Mr. French's Kitchen   29

John Williams was our "temporary" Mr. French. A truly gifted actor,
he worked with practically everyone in show business – including Cary Grant!

1 cup dry red wine
2 cups beef broth
2 tbl unsalted butter, softened
3 tbl all-purpose flour

In a small bowl whisk together the mustard, the garlic paste, the chopped rosemary, the chopped thyme, the soy sauce, the wine, and salt and pepper to taste. Add 2 tbls of the oil in a stream, whisking, and whisk the mixture until it is combined well. Brush the lamb generously on all sides with some of the mustard mixture, reserving the remaining mustard mixture, and let it marinate in a lightly oiled roasting pan, covered and chilled, for at least 6 hours or overnight.

Let the lamb come to room temperature and brush it with the reserved mustard mixture. In a bowl, toss the onions with 1 tbl of the remaining oil, add the onions and the carrots to the pan, and roast them with the lamb in the middle of a preheated 450° oven for 15 minutes. In the bowl, toss the potatoes with the remaining 1 tbl oil and add them to the pan. Reduce the heat to 350°. and roast the lamb and vegetables, stirring the vegetables occasionally, for 1 hour and 15 minutes, or until a meat thermometer registers 140° (for medium-rare meat). Transfer the lamb to a large platter and let it stand for 20 minutes. Transfer the onions and the potatoes with a slotted spoon to a serving dish, leaving the carrots in the pan, and keep them warm, covered.

Remove the string from the lamb, spoon some of the potatoes and onions around the lamb, and garnish the lamb with the thyme and rosemary sprigs. Serve the lamb, carved, with the gravy.

Making the gravy:

Pour off the fat from the pan, add the wine, and deglaze the pan over moderately high heat, scraping up the brown bits. Boil the mixture until it is reduced by half and strain it through a sieve into a saucepan, pressing hard on the carrots. Add the broth and bring the mixture to a boil. In a small bowl, knead together the butter and the flour until the mixture is combined well and add the mixture to the gravy a little at a time, whisking. Add any juices that have accumulated on the platter and salt and pepper to taste and simmer the gravy, whisking occasionally, for 3 minutes, or until it is thickened.

Steak Diane

Episode Thirty-Two: First Love

Although this episode does not center on food, I believe it has more references to different gourmet dishes than any other. Mr. French had his hands full this week, as did Sebastian Cabot, who had to remember all these names!

Ingredients:

1 (16-oz. size) boneless shell steak (also called New York strip steak, short loin or sirloin strip)
Salt
Freshly ground black pepper
2 tbl unsalted butter, divided
3 tbl finely minced shallots
6 tbl cognac or other good brandy, divided
2 tbl dry white wine or dry vermouth
2 tsp Dijon mustard (preferably imported)
2 tbl A-1 steak sauce
½ cup beef broth

2 tbl heavy cream
2 tbl finely snipped chives

Trim all outside fat off the steak. The steak should now weigh about 12 oz.

Cut the steak in half horizontally, creating two 6-oz. steaks. Pound the steaks lightly to flatten them to ¼-inch thick. Season them liberally on both sides with salt and freshly ground black pepper.

Heat a 12-inch skillet until a drop of water dances on the surface. Add 1 tbl of the butter. As soon as the foam subsides, add the seasoned meat. Cook on each side for 1 minute. Remove to a plate. Immediately adjust the heat under the pan to low. Add the second tbl of butter and the shallots. Sauté the shallots for 1 minute. Increase the heat to high. Add 3 tbl cognac and flambé, if desired. Add the wine, and with a wooden spoon, scrape up any browning in the pan (deglaze the pan). Stir in the mustard and A-1 sauce. Cook for about a minute, or until the liquid is reduced to a syrup. Add the broth and continue to boil for about a minute, until reduced to a few tbl. Add the cream and stir well to incorporate. Boil a few seconds.

Taste for seasoning and add freshly ground pepper to taste. Add the remaining cognac and ignite. When the flames die down, stir in the chives, taste for salt and pepper, and adjust if necessary. Add the reserved steaks and their juices (that have accumulated on the plate) to the simmering sauce. Turn the steaks in the sauce a couple of times, as the sauce reduces a little more. Place the steaks on individual plates. Divide the sauce on the steaks. Serve with salad, mashed potatoes or brown rice, and some bread to mop up the sauce.

Celery Victor

Episode Thirty-Two: First Love

What can one say about celery? It is a crunchy, healthy and usually a boring part of our diets. Not so with this recipe, which takes celery into a new, tangy dimension!

Ingredients:

4 small bunches celery
2 tbls fresh lemon juice
1/3 cup white wine vinegar
1/8 tsp dried mustard
2/3 cup extra-virgin olive oil
12 butter lettuce leaves
16 anchovy fillets
Chopped fresh parsley

Remove outer celery stalks from each bunch, leaving about 6 inner stalks attached. Trim each celery heart to 6-inch length (reserve outer stalks and trimmings for another use). Bring large pot of salted water to boil. Add lemon juice, then celery hearts and boil until celery is tender, about 15 minutes. Drain well. Cover and chill until cold, about 2 hours.

Whisk vinegar and mustard in a small bowl. Gradually whisk in oil; season with salt and pepper to taste. Arrange lettuce leaves on four plates; add celery. Arrange four anchovies over each celery heart. Spoon dressing over hearts and top with parsley.

Asparagus Soufflé Recipe

Episode Thirty-Two: First Love

Asparagus and soufflés: two things many cooks try to avoid making. Naturally, they are brought together in this fancy recipe. The secret to tender and tasty asparagus is to hold the spear in your hands, one hand at each end. Snap the spear gently, and it will break exactly where the tasty, tender part ends and the firmer, bitter part starts. Please do not be afraid of this recipe – the batter can be made ahead of time and if you follow the directions, I assure everyone at your table will be quite pleased with the outcome!

Ingredients:
1lb asparagus spears, bottom ends trimmed and discarded, thick spears peeled, spears cut into 1-inch pieces
Salt
¼ cup chopped shallots
1 clove garlic, chopped
1 tsp fresh thyme, chopped or ½ tsp dried
4 tbl unsalted sweet butter
½ cup finely ground Italian breadcrumbs
3 tbls cake or all-purpose flour
1¼ cups whole milk or canned condensed milk
¼ tsp ground nutmeg

Pinch dry ground mustard
Pinch ground ginger
Pinch freshly ground pepper
3/4 cup grated Gruyere cheese
5 eggs, yolks separated from the whites
8-oz. ramekins

Blanch asparagus for 2 minutes in boiling salted water (1 tsp of salt for every quart of water). Drain. Rinse in cold water to stop cooking. Set aside to let cool. Melt 1 tbsp butter in saucepan on medium heat. Add shallots, garlic, and thyme. Cook gently until soft, do not let brown. About 4 to 5 minutes. Remove from heat.

Purée asparagus and shallot mixture in a blender. Measure out 1¼ cup of purée. Butter 6 8-oz. ramekins. Coat well with the breadcrumbs, reserving any leftover breadcrumbs.

Make a thick béchamel sauce. Over medium-low heat, melt 3 tbl butter in a medium-sized saucepan. Add the cake flour and whisk to completely incorporate the flour into the butter, continue to stir for a couple of minutes. Do not let brown. Very slowly, add the milk to the mixture, little by little, whisking constantly. Stir in ½ tsp of salt, the nutmeg, cumin, mustard, ginger, and some fresh ground black pepper. Lower the heat to low and let cook for 15 minutes, stirring occasionally to keep the mixture from sticking to the pan. After 15 minutes, remove the béchamel from the heat and stir in the cheese. Transfer the béchamel and the asparagus mixture to a large mixing bowl (if you have a mixing bowl with a pour lip on the side, use it, it will make it easier to pour out later). Taste the mixture and adjust the seasonings. The soufflé base should be well seasoned. Stir in the egg yolks until well combined.

At this point you can make ahead the soufflé mixture. Refrigerate to store for up to two days. Return to room temperature before proceeding. Preheat oven to 400°. Prepare to make a water bath. Have ready a 9x12 baking dish with at least 2-inch sides. Put on a kettle of water to boil. Add a pinch of salt to the egg whites and using a mixer, beat the egg whites to firm but soft, almost stiff, peaks. (Make sure there are no traces of egg yolk or shell in your egg whites before starting.) Do not over-beat. Over-beating results in stiff peaks that are dry, somewhat reminiscent of Styrofoam. Use a rubber spatula to first fold in one quarter of the beaten egg whites into the asparagus mixture, then the remaining three-quarters. Use a light touch to keep from deflating the egg whites.

Fill ramekins with the mixture up to a quarter-inch from the top. If you want, sprinkle leftover breadcrumbs on top. Place the ramekins in the baking dish. Place baking dish on the middle rack in the oven. Pour boiling water into the baking dish around the ramekins until the water comes up halfway the sides of the ramekins. Bake for 10 minutes at 400°F, reduce the heat to 350°F and bake for about 15 minutes more, until puffed up and golden brown. Don't open the oven door until the soufflé is just about done, or it may fall. Serve the soufflés immediately!

Blintzes

Episode Thirty-Seven: Fat, Fat the Water Rat
Religion was discussed rarely on the show, but respect for others with different backgrounds was a hallmark. Jackie Coogan, a child star since the days of silent films, was our guest for *Fat, Fat the Water Rat*. Unprotected by any child labor laws, when Jackie became an adult, he found that his family had squandered his fortune. Because of his experiences as a child, and through the

efforts of child activists such as Paul Petersen with his organization A Minor Consideration, child actors today have better (although still not great) protections for safety, schooling and finances. Long after Jackie was considered a top movie star, Mr. Coogan made a fine living as a character actor on television. You may remember him as Uncle Fester on *The Addams Family* or for his appearances with Lucille Ball on her shows. He was a doll!

Jody was so enamored of this Jewish blintz delicacy (served to him by his first Hebrew friends) that Mr. French put the recipe into his own repertoire. While cheese and fruit blintzes are the most popular today, the classic version is potato.

Ingredients:
2 eggs well beaten
1 cup flour
½ tsp salt
1 cup whole milk or canned condensed milk
4 potatoes peeled and boiled until a fork pierces easily
2 onions finely-chopped and sautéed until almost caramelized
1 large egg lightly beaten
Salt and pepper
1 cup sour cream

Make batter by adding salt, sugar, and milk to eggs stirring well to blend; gradually add flour (tip: replace 1/3 of the flour with potato starch for a very smooth batter), stirring until smooth. Heat a 6" to 7" skillet, over moderately high heat, greased lightly. Pour in sufficient batter to thinly coat the bottom of the pan (1 to 2 tbl), quickly rotate the pan to distribute batter evenly, pour excess batter back into bowl. Cook until the batter sets and the edge of the pancake starts to leave the sides of the pan. Turn out onto a clean cloth and repeat until all batter is used, greasing pan when needed. Regulate the heat and frying time so that each pancake will cook to a uniform pale gold color.

Potato filling: In a food processor, combine potatoes, onions, 1 egg, salt and pepper until combined.

Filling the blintzes: Place a tbl of filling in the center of the cooked side of the pancake and fold over to make a square pocket or place filling at one end of the blintz leaf and roll up encasing the filling. Fry the blintzes on all sides until golden. Serve with sour cream.

Fillet of Beef Wellington with Pate de Fois Gras

Episode Forty: You Like Buffy Better

This episode introduced handsome Gregg Fedderson to the show. Although he appeared here as Ronnie Bartlett, he would eventually be called Gregg and become Cissy's boyfriend for the rest of the series. When I tell you that Gregg was not only great looking but also charming and good company, I will also have to admit that we began to date in our private lives as well and became very close. Was he a great actor? No, but he was very appealing and he was the son of the man who owned *Family Affair*, Don Fedderson. Unfortunately, Don did not approve of our off-camera relationship, and for a while the character of Cissy was featured a little less often. Gregg and I had great experiences together, but sometimes when we had a scene, "One take Kathy" would have to repeatedly do the lines over because of giddiness! Tragically, Gregg was involved in an accident not long after the show went off the air. Comatose for several years, Gregg finally passed away at a very young age. It was a huge loss for all of us who knew him and loved him.

Ingredients:
3½ lb fillet of beef tied with thin sheets of larding fat at room temperature
3/4 lb mushrooms, chopped fine
2½ tbl unsalted butter
½ lb pâté de foie gras (available at specialty foods shops) at room temperature
Note: If you cannot find it in your locality, substitute chopped chicken livers or any other pate you enjoy; making sure it is finely chopped and well-spiced
1 lb puff paste or thawed frozen puff pastry plus additional for garnish, if desired
1 large egg white beaten
Egg wash made by beating 1 large egg yolk with 1 tsp of water
½ cup Madeira
2 tsp arrowroot dissolved in 1 tsp cold water
½ cup beef broth
2 tbl finely-chopped black truffles (available at specialty food shops), if desired
Watercress for garnish, if desired

In a roasting pan roast the beef in the middle of a preheated 400° oven for 25 to 30 minutes, or until the thermometer registers 120°. Let the fillet cool completely and discard the larding fat and the strings. Skim the fat from the pan juices and reserve the pan juices.

In a heavy skillet cook the mushrooms in the butter over

Handsome Gregg Fedderson and I attend a party together.
His premature death was an enormous loss.

moderately low heat, stirring, until all the liquid they give off is evaporated and the mixture is dry. Season them with salt and pepper, and let them cool completely. Spread the fillet evenly with the **pâté de foie gras**, covering the top and sides, and spread the mushrooms evenly over the **pâté de foie gras**. On a floured surface roll 1 lb of the puff paste into a rectangle about 20 by 12 inches, or large enough to enclose the fillet completely. Invert the coated fillet carefully under the middle of the dough, and fold up the long sides of the dough to enclose the fillet brushing the edges of the dough with some of the egg white to seal them. Fold ends of the dough over the fillet and seal them with the remaining egg white. Transfer the fillet, seam side down, to a jelly-roll pan or shallow roasting pan and brush the dough with some of the egg wash. Roll out the additional dough and cut the shapes with decorative cutters. Arrange the cutouts on the dough decoratively, brush them with the remaining egg wash, and chill the fillet for at least 1 hour and up to 2 hours. Bake the fillet in the middle of a preheated 400° oven for 30 minutes, reduce the heat to 350°F and bake the fillet for 5 to 10 minutes more, or until the meat thermometer registers 130°F for medium-rare meat and the pastry is cooked through. Let the fillet stand for 15 minutes.

In a saucepan, boil the reserved pan juices and the Madeira until the mixture is reduced by one fourth. Add the arrowroot mixture, the broth, the truffles, and salt and pepper to taste and cook the sauce over moderate heat, stirring, being careful not to let it boil, for 5 minutes, or until it is thickened. Loosen the fillet from the jelly-roll pan, transfer it with two spatulas to a heated platter, and garnish it with watercress. Serve the fillet, cut into 3/4-inch-thick slices, with the sauce.

Torte Macaroon

Episode Forty-One: Freddie

As sometime happens, *Family Affair* was pre-empted a couple of times during its first season for special programming. Rather than extend the season, this episode was held over and shown during the second season. It is a bit unnerving to suddenly find Buffy, Jody and Cissy a year younger when watching these shows in order!

Ingredients:
¼ cup brown sugar
1 tsp minced fresh ginger
1 ½ tbls lime juice
3 large ripe mangos
1 cup blanched whole almonds
½ cup matzoh meal
¾ cup white sugar
½ tsp vanilla
½ tsp grated lime zest
3 egg whites

Preheat oven to 350°, then lightly grease a round cake pan. Put brown sugar, ginger and lime juice in a prepared pan and place over low heat. Cook, stirring until brown sugar melts and comes to a simmer, and then remove from heat. Core, peel and cut mangos into ¼" slices. Arrange slices over sugar mixture in pan in concentric circles. Place over low heat and simmer 8 minutes, then remove from heat and set aside. Place almonds in food processor and process until paste forms. Add matzoh meal, white sugar, vanilla and lime zest, then process until combined. In a small bowl, whisk egg whites until frothy, then add to food processor and process until smooth. Carefully spread almond mixture over the mangos and bake 30 minutes. Place on a wire rack and let cool in pan 20 minutes. Run a knife around edge of pan to loosen, then invert onto a cake plate. Let cool completely before serving.

Southern Fried Chicken

Episode Forty-Three: Somebody Upstairs

How could anyone not like Joan Blondell? She had been a big movie star at Warner Brothers in the 1930s, been married to Dick Powell and was a much sought-after guest star on television when she worked with the cast of *Family Affair*. Miss Blondell had all the bombast of Ethel Merman and was a total trouper.

The musical number Anissa and I performed in this episode was done live on the set by us; we did not pre-record it nor was it dubbed by others. We both loved the opportunity to cut loose and show off our musical talents. I had studied piano and I enjoyed tickling the ivories. Buffy mentions that fried chicken is her favorite dinner, so Mr. French naturally had his own recipe. He claimed that deep-frying stained his butler's vest, so he created his own version that was both crispy and somewhat spicy!

Ingredients:
1 broiler – fryer chicken cut into 8 pieces
½ cup fine dry Italian breadcrumbs
½ cup grated Romano cheese
1 tsp salt
1 tsp seasoned salt

44   The Family Affair Cookbook

A loving moment with Sebastian and Johnny and Anissa.

Recipes from Mr. French's Kitchen   45

Our Mr. French with that delightful look of frustration on his face!

¼ tsp dried cumin
½ tsp dried tarragon
½ tsp dried dill weed
½ tsp oregano
1 tsp paprika
¼ tsp pepper
¼ tsp cayenne pepper (optional)
¼ cup extra virgin olive oil or melted butter

Wash chicken pieces; pat dry. Combine breadcrumbs, cheese, salts, paprika, herbs and peppers. Brush each piece of chicken with oil or melted butter, and then roll in crumb mixture. Place coated chicken pieces in shallow, lightly oiled baking pan, skin side up. Bake at 425° for about 35 to 45 minutes, or until chicken is tender and juices run clear.

Applesauce Cake:

Episode Forty-Six: Family Reunion

This is one of two episodes where the Davises go back to Terre Haute to visit the places where the children were born and lived before the accident that took their parents. To this day, I am teased by fans that live in this city that we mispronounced its name, which should sound something like *Terra Howt*. Mea culpa to all of you lovely people that call Indiana your home!

Ingredients:

2½ cups all-purpose flour
1 cup sugar
¼ tsp baking powder
1½ tsp baking soda

1½ tsp salt
3/4 tsp cinnamon
½ tsp ground cloves
½ tsp allspice
½ cup shortening, softened
½ cup water
16 oz. applesauce, unsweetened
1 large egg
½ cup nut meats, broken
1 cup raisins cut up

Preheat oven to 350°. Sift together flour, sugar, baking powder, baking soda, salt and spices. Add shortening and water and beat for 2 minutes. Add applesauce and egg and beat for 2 minutes more. Fold in nuts and raisins. Pour batter into a greased 12-by-7½-inch pan. Bake for 45 to 50 minutes. Cool. Top with your favorite lemon frosting, if desired.

Hot Chocolate:

Episode 104: Marooned

You might notice that the episode numbers jumped quite a bit between the last recipe and this one. So was I, as I watched every episode in order. Despite the heavy emphasis on Mr. French's cooking in the first two seasons, his culinary skills were rarely referred to starting in season three. Oh, we'd see him chopping vegetables or stirring some mystery concoction in a pan, but the names of dishes were not mentioned. Although Mr. French did serve the Davis family scrambled eggs, oatmeal and cold cereal, I didn't think you needed a cookbook for those recipes.

I didn't think you needed a cookbook for *this* recipe either, but it is the most fondly remembered (and most often asked-about) thing Mr. French ever prepared in the entire series! Many of you may remember the episode: Mr. French and Buffy and Jody are marooned in a cabin in New England during a blizzard. Being the perfect gentleman's gentleman, good old Giles made hot chocolate for the kids out of snow and a chocolate bar! I want to share with you a recipe that is *slightly* more sophisticated, both in its ingredients and preparation.

Ingredients:
1/3 cup unsweetened cocoa powder
¾ cup white sugar
1 pinch salt
1/3 cup boiling water
3½ cups milk
¾ tsp vanilla extract
½ cup half-and-half

Combine the cocoa, sugar and pinch of salt in a saucepan. Blend in the boiling water. Bring this mixture to an easy boil while you stir. Simmer and stir for about 2 minutes. Watch that it doesn't scorch. Stir in 3½ cups of milk and heat until very hot, but do not boil! Remove from heat and add vanilla. Divide between 4 mugs. Add the cream to the mugs of cocoa to cool it to drinking temperature. OR ... during a winter snowstorm, get some snow, melt it with a chocolate bar, heat it up and serve it!

Rock Cornish Game Hens

Episode 109: Wouldn't It Be Loverly

Strange as it may seem, Rock Cornish game hens did not exist before the 1950s. Although there is some contention as to who actually cross-bred different fowl to get this delicious bird, it was something new and terribly sophisticated when Mr. French served it in the 1960s. Usually served stuffed, the very small size allowed each guest to have their own bird (or even two!) served individually on a plate, without having to cut up a chicken or other fowl into pieces. My recipe has a tangy stuffing that will have your guests asking for more!

Ingredients:
6 to 8 oz. Bulk pork sausage
2 cups cornbread stuffing from a box
½ cup chopped apples
½ cup chopped pears
½ cup thinly sliced celery
¼ cup raisins
1/3 cup chopped onion
¼ cup grated Romano cheese
½ cup mushrooms, sautéed
¾ cup melted butter
2 tbl chicken broth
¼ tsp crumbled dried sage
¼ tsp poultry seasoning
¼ tsp sea salt
Dash pepper
1 tbl curry powder
2 tbl fresh lemon juice
6 Rock Cornish Game Hens

Brown sausage well; drain off all the grease. Add cornbread, apples, pears, celery, raisins, mushrooms, onion, Romano cheese, ¼ cup of the melted butter and 3 tbl chicken broth. Lightly stuff hens with dressing mixture and secure drumsticks with twine. Place hens in large roasting pan and bake at 400° for an hour, until the hens are tender. Baste hens while cooking with remaining butter, broth and lemon juice.

Canapés

Episode 126: The Unsinkable Mr. French

For more than a century, canapés have been the hors d'ourves of preference at any fancy gathering. Naturally, Mr. French served them any time Uncle Bill had business guests or wanted to impress a lady fair. Usually, they are some mixture of soft cheese, fish and garnish on a cracker or cocktail bread. The ultimate version is caviar topped with chopped egg and chopped onion. My version is for those of us without caviar budgets; your guests will beg you for this recipe!

Ingredients:
2 bricks cream cheese, softened at room temperature
3 scallions, finely chopped
6 oz. pimento-stuffed olives, finely chopped
½ cup shredded sharp cheddar cheese
½ cup grated Romano cheese
¼ cup real bacon bits
½ lb shrimp, finely chopped
2 anchovy fillets, drained and finely chopped

3 tbl any tomato-based hot sauce
2 tbl finely-chopped parsley
Sliced radish and julienned hothouse cucumber (cut into ½-inch pieces) for garnish

Add softened cream cheese and all ingredients in a mixing bowl. Cover with plastic wrap and refrigerate for at least three hours. Arrange cocktail bread on a fancy platter, covering each slice with the mixture. Garnish with the radish and cucumber.

Crown Roast of Lamb

Episode 130: Nobody Here But Us Uncles

A crown lamb roast is nothing but two racks of lambs tied together to create a crown! Ask your butcher to assemble it for you. Be sure to also ask him to remove the skin.

Ingredients:
2 racks of lamb, trimmed of fat and assembled and tied into a crown
¼ cup extra virgin olive oil
2 tbl fresh lemon juice
1 cup apricot marmalade
2 tbl mint jelly
1 tsp sea salt
1 tsp black pepper

Preheat oven to 475°. Create a marinade using lemon juice, olive oil, salt and pepper. With a brush, baste it on lamb racks. To help keep its crown shape, place an oven-proof bowl or small dish in the middle of the crown. If you do not have one, a large wad of foil will also do the trick. You must cover the bones that are exposed at the top to prevent burning. Cover each exposed bone portion with foil. Place in shallow roasting pan and bake for 20 minutes. Reduce heat to 325°. Baste lamb with marinade. Allow lamb to cook an additional 5 -10 minutes for rare, 10-15 minutes for medium-rare.

Laughter is the emotion as Sebastian, Johnny, Anissa and I pose together during our third season.

Recipes from Mr. French's Kitchen 53

Sebastian with the kids at the Ice Capades.

A posed Christmas shot taken during our third season.

Mid-Century Recipes for the Rich and Famous

Appetizers, Salads and Soups:

Oysters Rockefeller

Here is a dish that was on the menu of every fancy restaurant in the 1960s; it is now rare to find it even mentioned. I find this strange, because oysters are still so popular in seafood bars and sushi restaurants.

Ingredients:

Two dozen fresh oysters on the half shell, oyster liquor reserved
4 sprigs flat-leaf Italian parsley
4 green onions (including the green part)
A handful of fresh celery leaves
At least 6 fresh tarragon leaves
At least 6 fresh chervil leaves
½ cup dried fresh French breadcrumbs (homemade, not out of a can)
12 tbl unsalted butter, softened (hey, it's supposed to be "rich enough for Rockefeller"!)

Salt and freshly ground black pepper, to taste
Tabasco or Crystal hot sauce, to taste
2 tbl Pernod (optional)
Rock salt or kosher salt

Mince together the parsley, green onions, celery leaves, tarragon and chervil as finely as you possibly can. Take as much time as you need. Mince them more finely than anything you've ever minced in your life. Mix this together with the breadcrumbs and the softened butter into a mortar and mix the whole thing together into a smooth paste, but do leave a little texture to it. (You can do this in a blender or food processor, but you'll leave a lot of it behind, stuck to the inside, and it'll be just easier to do it by hand in a mortar; you'll have an easier time getting it all out, and you'll have the satisfaction of serving something truly hand-made.) Season the mixture to taste with salt and pepper, hot sauce and, if you like, the Pernod.

Preheat your broiler. Lower the top rack to the middle of the oven. Spread the rock salt (preferable) or kosher salt over a large baking sheet; this will keep the oysters level under the broiler, so that they won't tip over. Moisten the salt very slightly. Plant the shells in the salt, making sure they're level. Place one oyster in each shell, plus a little bit of oyster liquor. Spoon an equal amount of the prepared herb/butter mixture over each oyster.

Place the baking sheet on the middle rack and broil until the edges of the oysters have curled and the herb butter is bubbling, about five minutes. Watch carefully to make sure you don't overdo it. Serve immediately.

21st-Century Upgrade: Eliminate the hot sauce and instead use finely-chopped chipotle peppers.

Clams Casino

Clams have always been the oyster's poorer cousin. This is such a simple dish, and a great way to start an evening's festivities!

Ingredients:
24 live Clams
1 large Garlic clove, minced
4 tbl Green Peppers, chopped
8 tbl Butter
1 tbl Lemon Juice
6 tbsp seasoned Breadcrumbs

Preheat oven to 450°. Open clams and discard top shell. Place clams in a shallow baking pan. In a saucepan, melt 4 tbl butter and sauté the garlic and green pepper for 2 to 3 minutes. Add remaining butter, lemon juice, and breadcrumbs, mixing thoroughly. Place 1 tsp of mixture on top of each clam and bake for 10 minutes.

21st-Century Upgrade: Before baking, sprinkle clams liberally with Jack Daniels.

SALMON MOUSSE

From gelatins to aspics, it was once *very* fashionable to serve food that did the "shimmy-shake" on the plate. There are many such recipes I would not recommend, but this one is yummy!

Ingredients:
1 envelope of unflavored gelatin
¼ cup cold water
½ cup boiling water
½ cup mayonnaise (not mayonnaise dressing, but REAL

mayonnaise, Mr. French says. He says *Best Foods* is
"Best" — *Hellmann's* east of the Mississippi)
1 tbl lemon juice
1 tbl finely grated onion
Dash of Tabasco
¼ tsp sweet paprika
1 tsp salt
2 tbl finely-chopped dill
2 cup finely flaked poached fresh salmon or canned salmon,
skin and bones removed
1 cup heavy cream

Soften the gelatin in the cold water in a large mixing bowl. Stir in the boiling water and whisk the mixture slowly until gelatin dissolves. Cool to room temperature. Whisk in the mayonnaise, lemon juice, grated onion, Tabasco, paprika, salt and dill. Stir to blend completely and refrigerate for about 20 minutes or until the mixture begins to thicken slightly.

Fold in the finely flaked salmon. In a separate bowl, whip the cream until it is thickened to peaks and fluffy. Fold gently into the salmon mixture. Transfer the mixture to a 6-8-cup bowl or decorative mold (Mr. French like to use a copper mold of a fish). Cover and chill for at least 4 hours. Serve on toasts, black bread or crackers. Sometimes, Mr. French served the salmon mousse as a first course garnished with watercress for a special dinner when Uncle Bill had a date!

For an added treat the twins would ask for cucumber sauce to be served with the mousse - it made it extra rich but also extra good!

Cucumber sauce:
1 Large cucumber
3/4 cup heavy cream or cultured sour cream
¼ t Salt
1/8 t paprika

Pare, seed and finely chop the cucumber. Drain well on paper toweling. While draining, beat the cream and add the salt and paprika. Mix with cucumber and serve with mousse.

21st-Century Upgrade: add ¼ cup flavored vodka to the cucumber sauce, along with some capers.

EGGSTRAVAGANZA (DEVILED EGGS)
For some reason, rich or poor, almost every culture serves some form of this dish. It is zesty, fun to eat and fun to make!

Ingredients:
6 small eggs, cold
2 ¼ tbl sea salt (divided use)
¼ cup sour cream
3 tbl onion, minced
 2 tsp lemon juice
½ tsp lemon juice
½ tsp lemon zest, minced
½ cup high-quality black caviar
24 (3/4-inch) chive tops

Put the eggs in a medium saucepan and add enough water to cover them by more than 1½ inches. Add 2 tsp of the salt. Bring to a boil over high heat. Remove from the heat, cover and let sit for 12 minutes. Pour out the hot water. Rinse the eggs under cold running water for 2–3 minutes. Pour out any excess water and shake the pan, rolling the eggs so that they collide and the shells crack (Jody thought this was a GREAT game to play – crack the eggs for ten points). Cover with cold water. Peel under running water, rinsing off any remaining bits of shell.

Cut a thin slice off the top and bottom of each egg, being careful not to cut into the yolk. Cut the eggs in half crosswise. Remove the yolks and place in a small bowl. Arrange the white on a serving platter. Combine the yolk with the sour cream, onions, lemon juice, lemon zest and the remaining ½ tsp salt in a small bowl using a fork. Mash until creamy and well blended.

To ASSEMBLE:
Place yolk mixture in sealable plastic bag and squeeze into one corner. Cut a ¼-inch tip off the corner and pipe even amount into the egg white until filled. Top each egg with ¼ tsp caviar garnish with 2 chive tips set in a crisscross design. Serve immediately.

21st-Century Upgrade: Add 2 tsp Dijon mustard or bacon bits to the egg yolk mixture.

Salad Nicoise
This delicious salad was a staple at all of the better restaurants at lunchtime. The flavors are a unique mixture, the dish is not heavy, and it is calorie-friendly for those watching their figures.

Ingredients:
6 small New Potatoes
1 lb green beans
½ lb mixed greens

1 cup artichoke hearts
6 tomato wedges
3 hardboiled eggs, halved
½ cup black olives
1 (6-oz.) can tuna packed in water

Vinaigrette:
3 tbl white wine vinegar
2 tsp Dijon mustard
1 tsp garlic, smashed with salt until paste
Pepper to taste
9 tbl extra virgin olive oil

In a bowl, whisk together white wine, Dijon, garlic, and pepper. Drizzle in olive oil while whisking constantly. Arrange salad decoratively on a platter. Drizzle with the dressing.

21st-Century Upgrade: Substitute ripe green olives stuffed with feta cheese for the black olives; enjoy a Dirty Martini with your Nicoise.

FLAMING SPINACH SALAD

This dish is "hot'! Not only is this impressive in front of company, but the taste is delicate and rich at the same time.

Ingredients:
2 bunches tender spinach leaves
Vinegar
1 bunch watercress
8 strips of bacon
4 tsp sugar
4 tsp wine vinegar

1 tsp Worcestershire sauce
1 lemon
Cognac

Wash the spinach in cold water with a little vinegar. Remove stems. Dry leaves on paper toweling and tear into pieces. Place in bowl with watercress leaves. Cut bacon in ½-inch squares and cook in a skillet. Add sugar, wine vinegar and Worcestershire sauce to pan. Heat mixture to a boil and strain dressing over leaves, leaving bacon in the skillet. Squeeze lemon over leaves, then toss. Drain dressing off the salad and place leaves on plates. Add cognac to the bacon, warm to ignite, and spoon over spinach. Mr. French did his theatrical best when he lit the warmed cognac and we all applauded his derring-do!

MR. FRENCH'S LEEK AND SAUSAGE TART
Mr. French served a chicory salad with vinaigrette for a great country Sunday supper with this dish.

Ingredients:
1 10-inch tart shell, pre-baked
2 tbl dry breadcrumbs, mixed with
2 tbl freshly grated Parmesan cheese
1 12 oz. package bulk sausage, sautéed, crumbled, and
    drained on paper toweling
2 tbl unsalted butter
6 leeks, sliced
3 eggs
2 egg yolks
1½ tsp Dijon mustard
1 tsp salt

½ tsp cayenne pepper
1/3 cup melted butter
1/3 cup freshly grated imported Swiss cheese
2½ cup milk
½ cup freshly grated Parmesan cheese

Place baked tart shell on baking sheet. Sprinkle the bread crumb-cheese mixture on the bottom of the tart shell, and then add the sausage. Melt 2 tbl of butter in saucepan. Add leeks and cook until soft. Combine eggs and egg yolks and whisk. Stir in seasonings, melted butter, Swiss cheese, milk and cooked leeks.

Spoon mixture into the prepared shell and top with the ¼ cup parmesan cheese. Bake at 350° for 20 - 25 minutes or until knife inserted into the center comes out clean to indicate the custard is cooked. Serve warm.

21st-Century Upgrade: Substitute goat or feta cheese for the Swiss, grated Romano for the Parmesan, and add ¼ cup dark ale.

THREE ONION SOUP WITH CROUTONS

This is not the French onion soup you might have been eating for years. It is a much more delicate and creamy version, without the layer of fattening cheese on top. It's a great way to warm up on a cold winter's night, or you can serve it cold in the summer.

Ingredients:
4 tbl sweet butter
2 cups finely-chopped yellow onions
4 large leeks, white parts only, well cleaned and thinly sliced
½ cup chopped shallots
4 - 6 garlic cloves, peeled and minced

4 cups chicken stock (Mr. French always made his own)
1 tsp dried thyme
1 bay leaf
Salt and freshly ground pepper to taste
1 cup heavy cream
3 scallions, trimmed, cleaned and diagonally cut into ½-inch pieces
Toasted Mr. French bread croutons*
Snipped fresh chives

Melt the butter in a pot. Add the onions, leeks, shallots and garlic and cook covered over low heat until the vegetables are tender and lightly colored (Mr. French did it about 25 minutes). Add stock, thyme and bay leaf and season to taste with salt and pepper. Bring to a boil, reduce the heat, and cook partially covered for 20 minutes. Pour the soup through a strainer set over a bowl; transfer the solids and 1 cup of the liquid to the bowl of a food processor fitted with a steel blade and puree. Return the puree and remaining 3 cups of liquid to the pot and set over medium heat. Whisk in the heavy cream and bring to a simmer. Add the scallions and simmer another 4 minutes or until they are tender.

Ladle into heated bowls and garnish with croutons of toasted Mr. French bread and snipped fresh chives.

Serves 4 - 6

* Two ways to make great croutons:

1. Melt butter in a large skillet. Sauté a bit of garlic in the butter, if desired add bread cubes (½-inch cubes) and sauté over medium heat until golden brown, drain on paper toweling.

2. Spread the ½-inch cubes on a baking sheet. Toast in a 400° oven, stirring occasionally until crisp and brown (10 - 15 minutes).

Main Courses:

Lobster Newberg

This is comfort food for the wealthy and alcoholic! While it is expensive to prepare, the flavors of the alcohol and other ingredients meld together in a most delightful way.

Ingredients:
3 cups diced boiled lobster meat
¼ cup unsalted sweet butter
¼ cup medium dry sherry
1 tbl brandy
1 ½ cups heavy cream
¼ tsp nutmeg
½ tsp salt
1/3 tsp white pepper
¼ tsp cayenne pepper
4 large egg yolks well beaten

Melt butter in heavy saucepan then cook lobster meat in butter over medium heat for 2 minutes. Add sherry and brandy and cook for 2 minutes more. Set meat aside and keep warm. Add cream to sauce mixture and reduce to 1 cup. Add salt, pepper, cayenne, paprika and nutmeg and lower heat to medium low. Beat egg yolks well and whisk into sauce to thicken slightly. Return lobster meat to the sauce and heat well. Serve over toast points.

21st-Century Upgrade: Eliminate the toast points and use cornbread or pita bread; replace the sherry with Frangelico liqueur.

Pheasant Under Glass

This poor dish has been the subject of more food jokes and puns than just about any other. The pheasant was served under a glass cover (as opposed to a silver one) because of its beauty and to keep the meat as moist and juicy as possible.

Ingredients:
2 Pheasant breasts
2 tbls freshly squeezed lemon juice
½ tbl Salt
½ tsp Pepper
3 tbls unsalted sweet butter
1 tsp Shallots; peeled, chopped
2 tbls Brandy
1/3 cup Dry white wine
1/3 cup Heavy cream
1 tbl cayenne pepper
1 tbl truffles or morels; cut into thin strips
    2 tbls Mushrooms; thin strips

Remove skin from pheasant breasts. Trim edges and flatten breasts slightly with a meat mallet. Rub breasts with 1 tbl of the lemon juice, and sprinkle with salt and pepper. Melt 2 tbl of the butter in a 9-inch skillet. When butter foams, add breasts and sauté 3 minutes on each side. Do not overcook. Make a shallow cut in one of the breasts with a sharp knife. The meat should be pink and the juice that runs out should be clear yellow. Remove breasts from skillet and keep warm. Add shallots to drippings and sauté until golden brown. Drain butter from shallots and reserve. Add brandy and wine and reduce to half its volume. Add cream and cayenne and reduce to half its volume again. Strain sauce, and add the remaining 1 tbl lemon juice, the remaining butter and cayenne. Mix truffles and mushrooms, and divide into 2 portions. Place warm breasts on a serving dish. Top each with truffles and mushrooms. Pour sauce over breasts and cover with a glass cover.

21st-Century Upgrade: Serve with garlic mashed potatoes and steamed haricots verts.

Coq au Vin

This dish was originally made from roosters (coq is French for rooster), but any good chicken will do. The alcohol bath the chicken stays in overnight assures deep flavor and an uncanny juiciness.

Ingredients:
1 dozen new potatoes cut in pieces
Bouquet of herbs: 2 sprigs of thyme and 1 bay leaf, tied all
    together with string
2 chickens cut into 8 pieces or more
½ bottle of full-body Burgundy red wine
6 bacon slices, diced
½ lb button mushrooms
1 dozen small white onions
2-3 cloves of garlic, mashed
2 carrots, peeled and quartered
Sunflower oil and unsalted, sweet butter

Parsley
Salt and pepper

A day in advance, clean and cut the chicken into 8 pieces or more. Pour half a bottle of red Burgundy wine over. Add the small white onions, the quartered peeled carrots and the herbs. Cover and put in the refrigerator. The next day, remove and drain the chicken and vegetables. Put the wine aside for later use. Brown the chicken pieces with oil in a skillet. Remove the chicken. Using the same skillet, add garlic to the vegetables and heat for a couple of minutes. Put the chicken, the potatoes and the vegetables in a large saucepan. Pour the wine and add salt and pepper. Bring to a boil at moderate heat. Cover and cook at low heat for 1 or 2 hours. Heat bacon, onion and mushrooms in a skillet until brown (10 minutes). When the chicken is ready, add bacon, onion and mushrooms in the pan, cook and stir for 2 or 3 minutes. Taste and correct the seasoning. Add parsley to the chicken when finished. Prepare rice or potatoes to serve with Coq au Vin.

    21st-Century Upgrade: Substitute a good Cabernet Sauvignon for the Burgundy.

Steak Tartar
I don't know who first thought of the idea of serving raw ground beef mixed with anchovies and herbs, but this is delicious, sensual and a wonderful way to try something new!

Ingredients:
2 anchovy fillets
2 garlic cloves, crushed
1 tsp capers

1 egg
2 tbl Dijon mustard
Salt to taste
Freshly ground black pepper
¼ cup extra virgin olive oil
1 lb freshly ground steak
¼ cup minced shallots
¼ cup chopped red onions
4 tbl chopped hardboiled egg
4 tbl finely-chopped fresh parsley
8 slices of bread, tossed in olive oil and pepper and toasted

In a small wooden mixing bowl, combine the anchovy, capers and garlic. Using the back of a fork, crush and form a paste. Add the egg and mustard. Whisk well; season with salt, pepper and Worcestershire sauce. Whisk in the oil, to form an emulsion. In a cold mixing bowl, combine the ground steak and shallots; season with salt and pepper. Add the emulsion and mix well. Form the tartar into 4-oz. rounds, about 1-inch thick. Place in the center of four cold plates. Garnish each with traditional garnishes. Serve with toast points.

    21st-Century Upgrade: Eliminate the toast points and use jalapeno-cheese foccacia bread.

Welsh Rarebit

Although this dish is sometimes referred to as Welsh Rabbit, it is a meatless cheese dish that resembles an alcoholic grilled cheese sandwich. It was often served as a late-night supper after the theatre, opera or ballet. I used to go to Dupar's Restaurant (located in Studio City) for lunch, escaping from the studio commissary to savor this tasty dish!

Ingredients:
2 cups Stilton or Colby cheese
2 cups crumbly bleu, feta, goat or similar cheese
2 tbl unsalted sweet butter
3 tbl flour
2 egg yolks, whisked
1 tsp dry mustard
1 ½ tsp Worcestershire sauce
1 tsp paprika
1 pinch chili powder
1 pinch cayenne pepper
1 cup ale or stout
12 slices of French bread
Chopped parsley and cherry tomato to garnish

In a saucepan, melt the butter over a medium heat and add the flour. Cook for 1 minute, stirring constantly. Add the eggs and stir for another 30 seconds. Slowly whisk in the ale, but do not let the mixture boil. Add half of both cheeses and stir until creamy; repeat with the rest of the cheese. Stir in the Worcestershire sauce, dried mustard, paprika, chili, cayenne pepper, salt and pepper. Toast the French bread lightly, cutting into points; spoon creamy mixture on top and garnish with parsley and tomato.

21st-Century Upgrade: to make this dish without alcohol, substitute ½ cup unsweetened iced tea mixed with 1 tbl curry powder. Try using ripe Haas avocado and sprouts as the garnish.

Fish in Papillote with Tomato Basil Beurre Blanc
Do not feel embarrassed if you cannot pronounce this dish – just think of the trouble I had *spelling* it! While most fish dishes today are simple, they used to be as complicated as rocket science.

Ingredients:
1 lb sole or orange roughy fish fillets
2 large leeks
1 zucchini
1 tomato
2 tbl butter
Salt
Pepper
Fresh Basil leaves
Aluminum foil

Preheat oven to 475°. Cut leeks 1" above white, then cut them in half and julienne. Sauté leeks in 2 tbl butter until they are soft and lose color. Put 2 tbl water in pan. Cover and steam 2-3 minutes. Tear foil in square pieces. Pile in leeks, then place two slices of tomato on top, then 4-5 slices of zucchini, then filet of sole on top of pile. Salt and pepper vegetables and fish. Place 2 fresh basil leaves on top. Crimp edges of foil. Put on cookie sheet bake at 475°, 5-8 minutes.

When cooked, slide onto plate, remove basil leaves and cover with tomato basil beurre blanc.

Tomato Basil Beurre Blanc
Ingredients:
¼ cup dry white wine
1½ sticks butter
2 shallots, minced
¼ cup white wine vinegar
1 tbl chopped basil
 Salt and pepper
1 tomato, sliced

Reduce vinegar and white wine with shallots to 3 tbl. Add butter piece by tiny piece, whisking all the time. Add basil and tomato and serve immediately over fish in Papillote.

Medallions of Lobster A L'Estragon

Lobster seems to be the one ingredient that never goes out of style. No matter how you make it, everyone seems to savor it! This recipe has been around for a long, long time!

Ingredients:
1 select lobster tail (Mr. French always got *the* best lobster from the seafood store)
2 cups white Zinfandel wine
2 tsp chopped fresh tarragon
½ tbl lemon juice
Salt to taste
White pepper to taste
½ lb butter
Garnish - Lemon zest.

Cut the select lobster tail into slices approximately ½-inch thick. Broil. Upon completion, cover with the following sauce:

Combine the Zinfandel wine, fresh tarragon, shallots and lemon juice. Place over medium heat until reduced by three-fourths. Add salt and white pepper to taste. Remove from heat and add butter, one tsp at a time, whisking after each tsp. After approximately ½ lb of butter, sauce will thicken to a heavy cream ready for the lobster.

21st-Century Upgrade: Substitute a mixture of apple cider and vermouth for the Zinfandel.

Desserts:

Pancakes Barbara

This is a 21st-Century Upgrade on a classic mid-century dish. Believe it or not, this sweet confection was served as a main course for dinner! For those of you are movie buffs, this dish was referenced in the classic film *The Women*.

Ingredients:
Pancakes
1 quart of ice cream, any flavor
1 cup of whipped cream
½ cup of blanched almonds
1 cup of hot chocolate sauce or hot fudge

Use your favorite pancakes recipe to make individual pancakes. Layer your favorite flavor of ice cream between the layers. Top the dish with whipped cream, blanched almonds and hot chocolate or hot fudge sauce.

Bananas Foster

Uncle Bill used to have Bananas Foster a lot for dessert – before the kids came along!

Ingredients:
2 tbl brown sugar
1 tbl butter
1 ripe banana, peeled and sliced lengthwise
Cinnamon
12 oz. banana liqueur
1 oz. white rum

Melt the brown sugar and butter in a flat chafing dish. Add the banana. Sauté until tender. Sprinkle with cinnamon; pour in the liqueur and rum and flame. Baste until the flame burns out. Serve over ice cream.

Poached Pears

Uncle Bill had Mr. French make these for special dates – the kids weren't invited!

Ingredients:
½ cup water
2 tbsp sugar
3 (¼-inch thick) slices ginger root
2 medium large pears, peeled, quartered, and cored
2 tbsp pear liqueur

Combine water, sugar and ginger root slices in heavy bottomed pan. Bring to boil. Add pear quarters. Reduce heat to low, cover and simmer until pears are tender – about 20 minutes. Remove pears and set aside in dish.

Return liquid to a boil and cook until syrupy and reduce by one third. Add pear liqueur. Pour liquid over pear and chill 1 hour. Remove ginger slices before serving.

Cherries Jubilee

The French seem to love foods that are set on fire, probably as much for the fun of it as for the flavor. This classic dessert was often the fore spice to an evening of romance!

Ingredients:

2 lbs sweet cherries, pitted and halved
2 tbl sugar
1 tbl cornstarch
2 tbl butter
¼ cup cognac
Vanilla ice cream (enough for 8 ½ cup scoops)

Sprinkle sweet cherries with 1 tbl sugar and let sit about 30 minutes to draw out the juices. Pour off the juice into a medium saucepan. Mix 1 tbl cornstarch with 1 tbl sugar. Add to juice and stir to combine. Add butter and about one-fourth of the cherries and mix well. Cook over low heat until the sugar has dissolved. Add remaining cherries and bring the mixture to a boil. While the pan is hot, remove it from the flame **(very important – please do not skip this step!)** of the stove and add the liquor. If your pan is hot enough, the liquor should ignite when you return it to the stove (if you are cooking on an electric stove, use a stick lighter or a long kitchen match). Gently shake the skillet over the hot burner until the flames die out. Much, but not all, of the alcohol will burn off. Serve warm over a scoop of ice cream.

21st-**Century Upgrade:** Substitute heavy, dark rum for cognac and substitute Ben and Jerry's Cherries Garcia flavor ice cream for vanilla.

Brian had the enviable reputation of being an appealing ladies man - Geraldine Brooks is shown here with Brian in an episode of The Virginian having a great time!

Uncle Bill's Libations and Potent Potables 77

Brian Keith on the set of Family Affair as he prepares to play Uncle Bill on one of his many romantic rendezvous in the Big Apple.

Uncle Bill's Libations and Potent Potables: Classic Cocktail Recipes from the 1960s

Cocktails are like trendy restaurants: they come and go as people discover them and then tire of them. While today's imbibers prefer cosmopolitans, mojitos and dirty martinis, in Uncle Bill's day the drinks of choice were much different and more varied. Good bartenders had to know dozens of recipes by heart, and good hosts had well-stocked bars in their homes. Since everything old is always new again someday, here are some recipes that you can enjoy when you are feeling either nostalgic, elegant, or want to start a new trend. If you've never tried them before, you are in for a surprise: these drinks are delicious and powerful! Serve them for any sort of get-together and your friends will think you are awesome! Make sure you have plenty of ice on hand, as well as the proper-sized glasses for the drinks. These may include a classic champagne glass (*not* flute), classic martini or cocktail glass, highball glass, rocks glass, Collins or sour glass. Make sure you have plenty of coffee cups!

Classic Champagne Cocktail

Ingredients:
3 oz. Champagne
1/3 oz. Cognac
2 dashes bitters
1 tsp sugar

Soak one sugar cube in a champagne glass with bitters. Add champagne and cognac. Squeeze in a twist of lemon and discard. Garnish with half a slice of orange.

Classic Martini

Ingredients:
2 ½ oz. gin or vodka
½ oz. dry vermouth
Green olive, lemon twist or pearl onion to garnish

Pour the ingredients over ice cubes into a mixing glass or shaker. Either stir briskly in the glass or shake briskly in the shaker. Strain liquid into martini glass and garnish. If you change the gin or vodka for scotch, you have made a classic *Rob Roy*.

Classic Eggnog

Ingredients:
1¼ oz. milk, condensed canned milk or half-and-half
½ oz. sugar syrup
1 oz. brandy, bourbon, Irish whiskey or rum (or combine smaller amounts of more than one to equal one oz.)

1 egg yolk
Dash of nutmeg

Pour the ingredients into a cocktail shaker filled with ice. Shake extremely well for twice as long as you would for most drinks. Strain into old-fashioned glasses or rocks glasses.

Classic Whiskey Sour

Ingredients:
1 ½ oz. of bourbon
1 ½ oz. freshly squeezed lemon juice
¾ oz. sugar syrup
Maraschino cherry for garnish

Pour the ingredients into a cocktail shaker filled with ice cubes. Shake very briskly and strain into chilled sour glasses. Garnish with cherry

Classic Manhattan

Ingredients:
2 oz. rye whiskey
½ oz. sweet vermouth
3 dashes of bitters
Maraschino cherry for garnish

Pour the ingredients into a mixing glass with ice cubes. Stir well. Drain into chilled cocktail glasses. Garnish with the cherry.

Classic Old Fashioned

Ingredients:
1 sugar cube
3 dashes of bitters
2 orange slices
3 oz. of bourbon or rye whiskey
Dash of club soda
Maraschino cherry for garnish

Place the sugar cube at the bottom of an old-fashioned or rocks glass. Saturate the cube with the bitters. Add one orange slice. Muddle these ingredients at the bottom of the glass using a spoon, pestle or whisk. Fill the glass with ice cubes. Add the bourbon or rye and stir well, allowing some ice to melt. Add the club soda, second orange slice and cherry.

Classic Sidecar

Ingredients:
1 ½ oz. Cognac
¾ oz. Cointreau
¼ oz. freshly squeezed lemon juice

Pour the ingredients into a cocktail shaker with ice cubes. Shake well and strain into a chilled cocktail glass.

Classic Highball

Ingredients:
2 oz. of whiskey
Ginger ale

Fill highball glass with ice cubes. Add whiskey, and then top with ginger ale.

Classic Gimlet

Ingredients:
2 oz. gin or vodka
1 ¾ oz. Rose's lime juice
Pearl onion for garnish

Pour the ingredients into a mixing glass with ice cubes. Stir well and strain into a chilled cocktail glass. Add onion for garnish.

Classic Tom Collins

Ingredients:
2 oz. gin
Sour mix
Club soda
Orange slice for garnish
Maraschino cherry for garnish

Pour the gin into a Collins glass filled with ice. Fill with sour mix. Shake by placing a tin or small plate over the glass, giving a couple of good shakes. Add a splash of club soda and garnish with the orange slice and cherry.

Classic Daiquiri

Ingredients:
1½ oz. light rum
¾ oz. freshly squeezed lime juice or Rose's lime juice
¼ oz. sugar syrup

Pour the ingredients into a cocktail shaker with ice cubes. Strain into chilled cocktail glasses.

Classic Cuba Libre

Ingredients:
2 oz. light rum
4 oz. freshly opened cola soda
Juice of half a large lime
Sliced squeezed lime

Squeeze the juice of half a lime into a Collins glass. Drop the half of the lime itself into the glass. Add ice cubes and pour in remaining ingredients. Stir well. Add other half of lime for garnish.

Buffy the cook!

Jody and Cissy enjoying a moment of nature.

Buffy and Jody Carefully check out the fresh crabs!

Buffy and Jody's Recipes for Children

Some of my fondest childhood memories center on the kitchen. Whether I was watching an adult cook or trying my wings at creating a culinary "messterpiece," the recollections are warm and vivid. Here are some time-tested recipes that kids love to eat and, even better, love to help make. As you will remember from *Family Affair*, Buffy and Jody pitched in with the cooking as soon as they could reach the sink.

Some of these recipes require adult supervision or an adult taking an active role (depending upon the children's ages); others are suitable for the kids to take over and the adults to just stand back and watch.

Main Courses:

JODY'S TURKEY WRAP

Jody would "gobble" up these turkey wraps after he helped Mr. French make them for his lunch.

Brian Keith loved working with children and it shows!

Ingredients:
4 tsp mustard (Cissy liked Dijon; Uncle Bill preferred mustard mixed with horseradish - Jody and Buffy were purists and used plain yellow!)
2 flour tortillas
2 slices American cheese, cut in halves.
½ cup shredded carrots (about 1 medium)
3 lettuce leaves, preferably romaine (I could never convince Jody the stiff leaves were better than iceberg), washed and torn into bite-size pieces.

Spread 2 tsp mustard over one flat tortilla; top with 2 cheese halves, half of turkey, half of shredded carrots and half of torn lettuce. Roll up tortilla and cut in half. Repeat with the rest of ingredients.

MR. FRENCH'S BAGEL PIZZA
Mr. French used to let Buffy and Jody make these tempting Italian treats for family movie nights around the television.

Ingredients:
1 cup shredded mozzarella cheese
1 tsp minced onion
½ tbl seasoned salt
Dash each of black and red pepper
Prepared pizza or spaghetti sauce
Bagels, sliced
Pepperoni, mushrooms, peppers, anchovies, sausage or olives

Put mozzarella cheese on the flat side of any flavor sliced bagel. Top generously with any other pizza ingredient and lots of pizza sauce. Put into toaster oven and broil until the cheese is completely melted.

Side Dishes:

Green Bean and Onion Ring Casserole

This book wouldn't be complete without this "classic" recipe that Buffy and Jody remembered from our days in Indiana when our parents were alive. Back then, this was something new and exciting that Mom served on special occasions. Who knew it would become an American classic? When we lived with Uncle Bill, Buffy and Jody would do all the mixing of the ingredients themselves; I helped them put it in the oven!

Ingredients:
2 packages frozen green beans, thawed
¾ cup canned condensed milk
2 cans condensed cream of mushroom or cream of celery soup
1½ cups French-fried onions
Salt and pepper to taste

In a greased 1½-quart casserole, combine all the ingredients except ¾ cup of French-fried onions. Bake at 350° for about 30 minutes. Top with remaining onions and bake until onions are golden brown, approximately five minutes.

For an autumnal take on this same recipe, substitute frozen sweet corn kernels for the green beans, cans of creamed corn for the canned soup and add ½ cup of grated Romano cheese.

Children are always curious, and child actors even more so!

Mishy Squishy Mashed Potatoes

I don't know any child that does not love mashed potatoes, even if all they do is play with them. No other cooked food has quite the same consistency, ease of swallowing and delight to a child's palate.

Ingredients:
9 large baking potatoes, peeled and diced
½ cup unsalted sweet butter, room temperature
12 oz. cream cheese, room temperature
¾ cup sour cream
½ tsp ground nutmeg
Salt and freshly ground pepper
Pinch of freshly grated nutmeg

Put the diced potatoes in a large saucepan and add water to cover. Heat the potatoes to boiling. Reduce heat and simmer over medium heat until drain and drain. Place the potatoes in a mixing bowl. Cut the butter and cream cheese into small pieces and add to the potatoes. Beat with an electric mixer or use a hand-held masher until light and fluffy. Beat in sour cream. Season with nutmeg, salt and pepper to taste. Serve immediately.

ANTS ON A BEAM
This is a simple one, but Jody loved it!

Ingredients:
½ head celery, separated into stalks
½ cup peanut butter
¼ cup raisins

Rinse celery twice. With a sharp knife (Mr. French did this part) cut the celery into 2-inch pieces. Spread the peanut butter into the celery pieces and let the kids put on the raisins - great and healthy snack! For variety, try cream cheese or pimento cheese – and try substituting olives, nuts or dried fruit for the raisins.

Mr. French Fries
Although Mr. French did not approve of the type of fries one got in fast-food restaurants, he was aware that they were considered haute cuisine in France and that the children (and Uncle Bill) loved them. Therefore, he made this version himself.

Ingredients:
6 russet potatoes, peeled
¼ cup of extra virgin olive oil

1 tbl salt
1tbl black or red pepper
1 tbl dill

Put oil in frying pan and heat on medium, being careful not to burn the oil or cause smoking. Slice the potatoes into 1/8-inch slices the short way. Carefully put the potato slices into the oil and season. Fry the slices until golden brown on both sides turning once, then remove from the pan and drain on a paper towel. Once drained, add additional seasoning as necessary and serve immediately with ketchup or your favorite salad dressing as a dip. Adult supervision is really needed for this one, as hot oil can burn badly!

Desserts:

Jody's Fave Banana Pudding
Even though this was Jody's favorite pudding, the twins would make it together – and also make a mess! This is definitely something that children can handle by themselves with very little supervision – but an adult should always be standing by just in case!

Ingredients:
1 large package instant vanilla pudding
2½ cups cold milk
1 can sweetened condensed milk
1 container whipped topping (16 oz.)
2 sliced ripe bananas
Vanilla wafer cookies

Anissa, Johnny and I having fun out on the town.

Mix pudding and milk; then add condensed milk. Blend well; fold in half the whipped topping. Alternate layers of pudding, bananas and vanilla wafers; top with remaining whipped topping and a few banana slices. Refrigerate overnight before serving.

Buffy's Fave Chocolate Pudding

Being a chocoholic, as soon as I knew Buffy was into her cocoa-laden creation, I would pop into the kitchen on the pretext of helping – and end up licking the bowl!

Ingredients:
3 squares unsweetened chocolate (3 oz.)
3 cups milk
¼ cup cornstarch

½ cup sugar
¼ tsp salt
1 tsp vanilla extract

In a saucepan, cook 2 2/3 cups of the milk with chocolate, stirring until chocolate is melted and milk is scalded. Mix cornstarch, sugar and salt in a bowl; stir in remaining 1/3 cup of milk. Add to scalded milk and chocolate mixture and cook over low heat, stirring constantly, until thickened and smooth. Continue cooking for about 5 minutes to thoroughly cook cornstarch. Cool slightly, stir in vanilla and pour into serving dishes. Let cool before licking the pan!

Cissy's Coconut Cookies
I'm no fool; these go great with Buffy's chocolate pudding!

Ingredients:
2/3 cup butter, softened
1 egg
½ tsp vanilla extract
½ cup packed light brown sugar
1 cup shredded coconut
2/3 cup rolled oats
1 cup self-rising flour
2 cups cornflakes, lightly crushed

Preheat oven to 325°. Grease 2 baking sheets. Put butter, egg, vanilla and sugar in a medium mixing bowl and beat until creamy. Stir in coconut, oats and flour and mix to form dough. Roll dough with your clean hands into about 24 balls, each one approximately about the size of a walnut. Put crushed cornflakes on a plate. Lightly press dough balls in cornflakes to coat. Place on baking sheets. Bake about 15 minutes until lightly browned. Transfer to a wire rack to cool.

TERRE HAUTE OATY FRUIT SURPRISES

The following recipe is a great way to get kids to eat hot cereal. Not only is it nutritious and warming, but also the kids can help with the preparations. This warm starter is just the type of breakfast Buffy and Jody had when they were very young in Indiana; Mr. French got the recipe from Aunt Fran.

Ingredients:
2 oranges
1 1/3 cups quick cooking oats
2 cups milk
1/3 cups raisins
1 tbl honey

Wash 1 orange and grate its zest. Squeeze out the juice and put it into a bowl with the zest. Remove the peel and white bitter pith from the other orange and cut into sections. Set aside. Place the zest, orange juice, oats and milk into a medium-size saucepan. Bring to a boil, stirring constantly. Reduce the flame to low and cook 1 minute. Stir in the raisins and honey. Pour into four serving bowls and decorate each with orange sections. Serve at once.

CISSY'S CARMEL APPLE CUT-UPS

Although this was hardly figure-friendly, I used to make this treat when I had a lot of studying to do and needed extra fuel.

Ingredients:
¼ cup peanut butter
2 tbl caramel topping
2 tbl milk
1 large apple, cut up or sliced thinly

Combine peanut butter, caramel topping and milk in small saucepan. Cook over low heat, stirring constantly, until mixture is melted and warm. Serve dip with cut up apples, or you can substitute celery or baby carrots. Buffy laughingly called Cissy a "cut up"!

PEANUT BUTTER S'MORES
This was the nearest the Davis Family usually got to camping.

Ingredients:
1½ cups all-purpose flour
½ tbl baking powder
½ tbl baking soda
¼ tbl salt
½ cup butter, softened
½ cup granulated sugar
½ cup packed brown sugar
½ cup creamy or chunky peanut butter
1 egg
1 tbl vanilla
½ cup chopped roasted peanuts
16 large marshmallows
4 (1.55 oz.) milk chocolate candy bars

Preheat oven to 350°. Combine flour, baking powder, baking

soda and salt in a small bowl; set aside. Beat butter, granulated sugar and brown sugar in large bowl of electric mixer at medium speed until light and fluffy. Beat in peanut butter, egg and vanilla until well blended. Gradually beat in flour mixture on low speed until blended. Stir in peanuts.

Roll dough into 1-inch balls. Place 2 inches apart on ungreased cookie sheets. Flatten dough with tines of fork, forming a crisscross pattern. Bake about 14 minutes or until set and edges are light golden brown. Cool cookies 2 minutes on cookie sheet. Transfer to wire cooling racks. Cool completely. To assemble sandwich cookies, break each candy bar into four sections. Place one section of chocolate on the flat slide of each cookie. Place on microwavable plate. Top with one marshmallow; microwave on HIGH 10 -12 seconds or until marshmallow is puffy. Immediately top with another cookie flat side down. Press slightly on top cookie, spreading marshmallow to edges. Repeat with remaining cookies one at a time. Cool completely.

And you WILL want "s'more"!

MR. FRENCH'S ENGLISH TOFFEE

Mr. French was a stickler that we eat proper foods and had quite a disdain for American candy. These crunchy treats were comfort food from *his* childhood, and everyone in the family enjoyed the sweets!

Ingredients:
2 cups sugar
3½ cubes of butter
1 cup sliced almonds
1 Large (8 oz.) milk chocolate bar
1 cup finely-chopped walnuts.

Blend sugar and butter in saucepan and cook on high heat for 7 minutes, stirring constantly. Add the almonds and cook another 5 minutes, stirring. Pour into greased jelly roll pan. Break apart the chocolate bar and put on the hot candy. Spread evenly when it melts. (Use more chocolate for a richer taste.) Sprinkle the walnuts over the chocolate. Let the candy harden; break into pieces.

The kids kept licking their fingers when breaking the candy into pieces, so Mr. French had to step in, with thin plastic gloves, to do the breaking the clean way!

DO IT YOURSELF SUNDAES

I had this for a dessert when Mr. French was in the park with the kids. My friends loved it - but they sure did make a mess!

You need to put out:
Bowls or sundae glasses or dessert glasses (with teenagers, plastic is good, too - they're not as sophisticated as they think!)
Spoons
Napkins!
Ice cream with scoopers
Nuts (pecans, walnuts, peanuts)
Sprinkles (Candy, cinnamon, silver)
Candies (M&Ms, chopped Snickers, etc.)
Cookies, crumbled (Oreos, peanut butter)
Sliced fruits (strawberries, blueberries)
Syrup: chocolate, butterscotch, maple, hot fudge
Cans of whipped cream (tell your guests not to shoot it at each other)
Cherries

Do I need to tell you what comes next? Just go for it!

Always with an open mouth!

Cissy in season one.

The smile is genuine in this third season photo: I loved what I was doing!

Cissy Sizzles: Kathy's Rousing Recipes

Appetizers, Salads and Soups:

Kathy's Kucumbers

This recipe was handed down through my family from my Grandmother Marie, who was from Austria and lived to be 101 years old! Her recipe lives on in this book – you see, it really is a family affair!

Ingredients:

1 cucumber (adjust ingredients below for each additional cucumber)
Salt to taste
2 tbls white or apple cider vinegar
3 chopped scallions
1 tsp sugar

Slice the cucumbers as thinly as possible. Put them in a bowl in layers and sprinkle each layer with salt. Cover the bowl and refrigerate for 2 to 4 hours. Some of the moisture will have drained out of the cucumbers. Wring out the remaining moisture and discard. Add the vinegar, scallions and sugar. Oil is not needed. Black pepper or red pepper flakes may be added to make the dish spicy.

This dish is a wonderful accompaniment to duck with red cabbage or any meat and potatoes meal. Thanks, Grandma!

GUACAMOLE

I have always loved ethnic foods, but could never figure out how to make a really good guacamole that was neither runny nor pasty. Thankfully, I was eating in a little café on a trip to New York City, and the guacamole there was the best I had ever tasted. Sometimes, being a celebrity helps – the chef came and sat with me and shared her recipe. Now I share it with you!

Ingredients:

4 or 5 large, ripe Haas avocadoes (they should be soft when touched but not mushy), peeled and mashed
5 cherry tomatoes, finely chopped
Finely-chopped red onion, enough to completely cover the palm of your hand
1 clove garlic, finely chopped
1 tsp cumin
1 tsp chili powder
½ tsp chopped fresh parsley
1 pinch sea salt
1 tbl grated pecorino Romano cheese
The fresh juice of one half of a lemon
Tabasco or your favorite hot sauce to taste

Fold all of your ingredients, one at a time, into the mashed avocado in the order listed, making sure to mix well but not to liquefy the avocado. If you like really spicy food, double the portions of chili powder, cumin and hot sauce. The guacamole should be stored in a bowl in the refrigerator for at least four hours before serving. Keep one or two of the avocado pits on top of the mixture and your dip will not turn brown. For variety, try adding a tbl of curry. This recipe is muy delicioso!

LIMESTONE LETTUCE SALAD

The older I get the more salads I eat and the more recipes I need to make them interesting. Here's one that's crunchy, tasty and a little different!

Ingredients:
3 bunches mache
2 bunches arugula
2 heads baby limestone lettuce
1 head baby radicchio
(Note: all lettuces, leaves separated and trimmed)
¾ cup walnut oil
1 lb each fresh chanterelle, shitake and oyster mushrooms, trimmed and cut into ½-inch pieces
½ oz. pancetta, cut into thin julienne strips (optional)
½ cup pine nuts
2 large shallots, finely chopped
2 medium cloves garlic, finely chopped
¼ cup sherry wine vinegar
2 tbls each minced fresh basil, tarragon, thyme and chives
Salt and freshly ground pepper to taste

Toss all greens together in a sizeable salad bowl. In a large sauté pan, heat 3 tbls of walnut oil over high heat until it just begins to smoke. Add the mushrooms and let them sear, without stirring, for about 30 seconds. Sauté them, stirring constantly, for about 2½ minutes more, until nicely browned. Add the mushrooms to the salad bowl.

To the same pan, still over high heat, add the remaining 1 tbl oil and sauté the pancetta for about 30 seconds. Add the shallots and stir them quickly, then add the garlic and sauté about 30 seconds more. Add the vinegar and stir and scrape to deglaze the pan, and then stir in the herbs, salt and pepper. Pour the dressing into the salad bowl and toss immediately to coat all the greens. Mound the mixture on salad plates and serve immediately.

CREAM OF RED BELL PEPPER SOUP

Yes, I know they are fattening, but creamed soups are divine! I have rarely seen peppers used in a soup quite this way, and I hope you get the same enjoyment slurping this delectable bisque that I do.

Ingredients:
4 red bell peppers, seeded and cut in pieces
Juice of ½ lemon
4 - 5 cups chicken stock
3 shallots, finely chopped
½ tsp salt
¼ tsp white pepper
3 tbl butter
3 tbl flour
½ - 2/3 cup half-and-half
Garnish - sour cream and chives

Combine peppers and lemon juice in bowl, set aside. In a medium saucepan, heat 4 cups of stock until simmering. Add pepper with lemon juice, shallots, salt and pepper. Cover and simmer 30 minutes.

Transfer pepper mixture to a blender or food processor using slotted spoon and add enough of the cooking liquid to cover; reserve remaining liquid. Puree until completely smooth. Melt butter in medium saucepan. Stir in flour and cook until light golden. Add reserved cooking liquid and pureed pepper mixture. Bring mixture to a boil and reduce heat and simmer 10 minutes, stirring constantly. Remove from heat and let cool slightly. Add half-and-half. Thin with additional chicken stock, if desired. Soup may be served hot or may be chilled for a cool summer soup. Sometimes, Mr. French would serve this to us out on the balcony on a steamy New York summer's day. He garnished it with sour cream and chopped chives. With the red and green - it was also good as a Christmas soup served hot in front of the fire!

SUMMER PASTA SALAD

This dish was first served by my friend Bronco Bill at the Tombstone American Legion Potluck. They couldn't get enough of it, so you know it is good!

Ingredients:
1 lb Pasta (Bill used Italian Gemelli)
1 green bell pepper, chopped
1 red bell pepper, chopped
6 green onions, sliced
3 oz. Black olives, chopped
1 can diced tomatoes (14.5 – 15 oz.)

2 oz. mushrooms (Bill used canned – Mr. French would use fresh!)
1 tsp minced garlic
¼ tsp fresh ground pepper
Salt to taste
Vinaigrette dressing (see recipe below)

Cook pasta to package directions; rinse and drain; cool down; add remaining ingredients; mix well. Add vinaigrette dressing. Mix well and chill 1½ - 2½ hours.

VINAIGRETTE DRESSING
Ingredients:
½ cup olive oil
½ cup canola oil
½ cup red wine vinegar
1½ tbl sugar
1 tbl granulated garlic
1 tbl parsley flakes
1 t granulated Onion
½ tsp ground Rosemary
½ tsp ground paprika
½ tsp ground chervil
½ tsp ground basil
½ tsp ground Oregano

Mix all ingredients well, and chill 1-2 hours. In a pinch, use 8-16 oz. bottle Italian dressing!

PATE DE LEGUMES (VEGETABLE PATE)

From my friend Charley comes this vegetarian version of pate. I do not know why so many people do not like liver; I love it! But if you are one of those who enjoy the idea of pate without the liver taste, this recipe is for you.

Ingredients:

9 eggs
2 lbs ripe tomatoes (about 5 large very red Italian tomatoes are best for color, Charley says)
2 lbs spinach
6 oz. (about 1 cup grated) fresh grated Parmesan, Romano or Swiss or mixture
2 cloves garlic, minced
½ tsp ground thyme (or 1 tbl fresh) can also use oregano
1 cup cream
½ cup olive oil or butter
2 shallots, minced or 2 tbl green onions, minced
Pinch of nutmeg and dry mustard
Salt and pepper to taste

Preheat oven to 350°. Boil water, drop in tomatoes for a few minutes and when skins pop, take out tomatoes and run cold-water over them. Peel tomatoes and chop pulp roughly into small pieces then drain liquid. Heat 2 tbsp oil in skillet, add tomatoes; add pinch of thyme, pinch of salt. Cook over high heat until all liquid is evaporated. Set aside to cool; should have 1 cup.

    Wash spinach thoroughly (3 times); remove tough stems only and drain as much as possible. Heat 2 or 3 tbl oil in large pot; toss spinach, garlic and shallots into pot and continue to toss as cooking. Add a pinch of salt and toss until all water is evaporated. Set aside to cool then drain thoroughly.

Cut a piece of waxed paper to fit in the bottom only of an 8" oven-proof bread-shaped pan and grease both sides of paper with butter, then fit it into bottom of pan so it sticks. Butter sides of pan, too.

Beat 3 eggs with 3 tbsp water then stir in chilled tomatoes and carefully pour into greased pan and bake at 350° for 15 minutes. Remove. (Note: you must put larger pan ½ filled with hot water and place greased pan with tomato mixture into water bath to cook.) After 15-20 minutes, remove pan. Make sure top isn't mushy.

Next, mix 3 beaten eggs with 1/3 cup sour cream and whipping cream mixture. Add 1 tsp dry mustard and mix in grated Parmesan/Romano cheese mixture (one cup) and then a pinch of white pepper.

Pour cheese mixture over tomato mixture carefully and cook another 15 minutes until almost set. Remove pan. Mix cooled spinach with 3 beaten eggs (note: chop spinach with a knife – spinach must be in small pieces before adding to eggs), then add 1/3 cup sour cream and whipping cream mixture, salt and pepper to taste and add dash of nutmeg. Pour spinach mixture carefully over cheese mixture. Cook another 20 minutes or until set: toothpick will come out clean. Allow to cool for about 10 minutes. Unmold on serving platter and serve hot. May be served totally cooled as hors d'ourves on crackers or party bread.

Main Courses:

CHICKEN MARENGO

This is an Italian savory dish, so named for being the dish that Napoleon Bonaparte ate after the Battle of Marengo.

According to tradition, Napoleon demanded a quick meal after the battle and his chef was forced to work with the meager results of a forage: a chicken (and some eggs), tomatoes, onions, garlic, herbs, olive oil, and crayfish. The chef cut up the chicken (reportedly with a saber) and fried it in olive oil, made a sauce from the tomatoes, garlic and onions (plus a bit of cognac from Napoleon's flask), cooked the crayfish, fried the eggs and served them as a garnish, with some of the soldiers' bread ration on the side. Napoleon reportedly liked the dish and (having won the battle) considered it lucky. He refused to have the ingredients altered on future occasions even when his chef tried to omit the crayfish.

Modern versions of the dish are made by first flouring, then browning chicken portions in oil or butter. The part-cooked chicken is then transferred into a tomato sauce (usually made with onions, garlic, wine and chopped tomatoes). The whole is then cooked slowly until the chicken is done, and a few minutes before serving, a good amount of chopped herbs and black olives are added. This would usually be eaten with a potato dish of some sort, or just crusty bread. Napoleon's name is associated with the origins of this dish. This one is truly yummy.

Ingredients:
1 large onion, finely chopped
Extra virgin olive oil
2½ to 3½ pounds chicken pieces or 1½ pounds boneless chicken breast cut into bite-size pieces
2 cans (14.5 ounces each) canned Italian plum tomatoes, drained
1 cup chicken stock
½ cup dry white wine or dry sherry
3 parsley sprigs
1 tbl ground thyme
1 tsp salt
½ tsp ground black pepper
1 bay leaf
2 cloves of crushed garlic
Butter
8 oz. sliced mushrooms
Juice of 1 lemon
2 tbl fresh minced parsley, for garnish

Sauté the onions in olive oil till translucent. Add pieces of chicken, sauté until brown on all sides. Add the tomatoes, the chicken stock and wine. Add the parsley sprigs, thyme, salt, pepper, bay leaf, and garlic. Simmer covered for 1 hour. Melt butter in a saucepan and sauté the mushrooms until tender. Sprinkle with lemon juice. Remove the chicken pieces from pot and arrange them in a dish. Strain the sauce. Add mushrooms to the sauce and pour over the chicken. Garnish with minced parsley and breadcrumbs. Serve with hot cooked pasta or rice.

FRESH SWORDFISH WITH OLIVADA

Some shark or swordfish may contain mercury, but if you just serve them every so often they make a special treat and can break up the monotony of salmon, sole and red snapper. This is a delicious way to serve a heavier fish.

Ingredients:

1 jar (8 oz.) Olivada Italian olive paste
6 swordfish steaks, 1-inch thick
1 cup Rouille (see recipe below)
1/4 cup parsley sprigs for garnish
6 lemon wedges

Preheat the broiler. Spread a thin layer of the Olivada on one side of each swordfish steak. Top with a thick layer of the Rouille. Place the steaks on a broiling pan and broil about six inches from the heat until browned, 6–8 minutes. Turn the steaks over and spread with another thin layer of the olive paste and a thicker layer of the Rouille. Broil until the fish is firm and cooked through, about 5 or 6 minutes. Place on a serving platter and garnish with parsley and lemon wedges

ROUILLE

Ingredients:

4 cloves of minced garlic
1 tsp of salt
1 tsp cayenne pepper
1 tsp sweet Hungarian Paprika
½ tsp saffron threads
1 tsp freshly squeezed lemon juice
2 egg yolks

¾ cup extra virgin olive oil
½ cup vegetable oil

Mash the garlic, salt, paprika, cayenne and saffron to a paste in a mortar and pestle or with the back of a spoon. Let stand 5 minutes. Whisk in the lemon juice and egg yolks. Add the oils (drops at first, then a thin stream), whisking all the time. The Rouille should be the consistency of mayonnaise. For a quicker Rouille, take some Best Foods (Hellman's Mayonnaise) and add some chopped garlic, paprika a little salt and some herbs de Provence. Saffron is getting to be very expensive these days!

BEVERLY'S VEAL SCALOPPINI

This is my real sister Beverly's, as opposed to my "reel" sister Buffy's recipe. She is a gourmet cook, and you will be, too, when you serve this delicious entrée.

Ingredients:

1/3 lb veal or two pieces per person of thin veal cut from the
    round (good) or leg (better)
½ cup flour
½ cup grated Parmesan or Romano cheese
Salt
Egg wash (1 egg plus 1 tbl water)
1 tsp extra virgin olive oil
2 tsp butter
1 can chicken broth
½ cup sherry
½ lb sliced mushrooms
2 tbl butter
1 tsp Italian seasoning

Pound the veal slices until quite thin. Mix equal parts flour and cheese. Sprinkle each slice of veal with salt on both sides; dip in the egg wash and then in the flour/cheese mixture. Heat olive oil and butter in a skillet and brown the veal. Add chicken broth and sherry to the veal. In a separate pan, put sliced mushrooms with no oil or butter. The mushrooms will exude their moisture. When they are dry, add butter and sauté until brown, and then add them to the veal. Season with Italian seasoning when adding mushrooms. Simmer 15 minutes.

CHICKEN MUSHROOM CASSEROLE

Today's busy households know the importance of nutritious meals that can be prepared in a short amount of time. The wonderful Rachael Ray is the diva of thirty-minute meals, but I wanted to include two of my own. This delicious chicken dish and the comfort food recipe that follows are ones I have been preparing for my own family for years.

The nice part of this one is that it calls for cooked chicken, so you can use leftovers from previous meals, cooked chicken you have sitting in the freezer (defrost first) or canned or packaged chicken. In the time it would take to go get fast food and bring it home, you can make these dishes and get the grateful applause of your loved ones!

Ingredients:
½ cup butter
1 cup sliced mushrooms
1/3 cup flour
2 cups chicken broth or chicken stock
1 cup milk
¼ cup pimento, chopped

2 tsp salt
½ tsp pepper
2 cups cooked diced chicken
1/3 cup grated Parmesan cheese
1 package egg noodles

Preheat oven to 350°. Cook noodles according to package directions and drain. In large skillet, melt butter over low heat; add mushrooms and sauté. Blend in flour, stirring until smooth. Gradually add broth, milk, pimento, salt and pepper, stirring constantly until sauce is thickened. In a buttered 2½-quart casserole dish, combine noodles, chicken and sauce. Sprinkle cheese over top and bake 20 to 25 minutes.

TUNA NOODLE CASSEROLE

I had to include this recipe! Sometimes even Mr. French was in a crunch for time and needed to whip up an easy and timely recipe (especially to the cries of Buffy and Jody, as this was one of their favorite dinners our mother made when we were very little!). Sophisticates Cissy and Uncle Bill enjoyed it as fondly-remembered comfort food, and even Mr. French gave it a hearty "By-Jove, sir" when he first tried it. The Garver/Travis family enjoys it as well, so this is one dish that reely and really belongs in this book!

If you don't want to use breadcrumbs, you can substitute crushed potato chips or grated cheese – or just leave it without a topping!

Ingredients:
8 oz. egg noodles, uncooked
1 can condensed cream of mushroom soup
½ cup milk

1 cup frozen peas
Chopped pimentos (optional)
2 cans tuna in water, drained and flaked
2 cups hot, cooked medium egg noodles
2 tbls dry breadcrumbs
1 tbl butter

Mix soup, milk, pimentos, peas, tuna and noodles in 1½-quart casserole dish. Bake at 400° for 20 minutes or until bubbling hot. Stir. Mix breadcrumbs with butter and sprinkle on top. Bake for five minutes more.

PORK CHOPS AND RICE

As a mother, wife and a busy actress (thank goodness!), I am a great believer in the family dinner table and hearty meals. This is the sort of down-home cooking we enjoy in our household, and I think everyone (with the possible exception of Mr. French) will savor it in theirs.

Ingredients:
1 ½ tbl butter
1 ½ tbl olive oil
1 cup matchstick carrots
8 oz. sliced mushrooms
½ cup chopped onion
2 ribs celery, sliced
6 to 8 boneless pork chops
⅓ cup white or blush wine
1 envelope pork gravy mix
1 cup water
2 to 3 cups cooked rice, heated

Preheat oven to 325°. Melt butter with oil in a large skillet over medium heat. Add carrots, onions and celery; sauté until just tender. Add mushrooms and sauté until mushrooms are browned. Add pork chops; cook, turning, until chops are browned. Add wine; simmer until wine has almost cooked off; stir in gravy mix. Add water and cook until thickened and bubbly. Place rice in a 2-quart casserole dish; top with chops, vegetables and sauce. Bake for approximately 20 minutes.

SWISS CHARD TORTA

As almost all women have found out, working and raising a family is not easy. It is a challenge for me to cook tasty, nutritious meals quickly. Breakfasts and brunches are especially difficult, because if I am home I want to sleep in, and if I am working I am not home. This recipe is wonderful, because it is yummy, good for you, easy to make and pleasing to my husband and son. What is even better, it is so easy, my men can make it themselves!

Ingredients:

1 onion, minced

Olive oil

2 tsp minced parsley

½ tsp each fresh thyme, marjoram, and oregano (or 1 tsp of dried Italian seasoning if a son forgot to water the fresh herbs out on the patio)

1 cup cooked chopped Swiss chard, squeezed dry

2 slices bread, soaked in milk, squeezed almost dry

2 cups grated parmesan or dry jack cheese

6 beaten eggs

Salt and pepper to taste.

Sauté the onion untill lightly browned: Add the herbs and cook a minute longer. Cool. Blend everything together, mixing well. Pour into an oiled shallow baking pan; bake at 350° for 30 minutes or till lightly browned. Serve hot or cold depending on when *your* Uncle Bill gets home.

ELEGANT CRAB STRUDEL

Elegance is not a word one hears too often anymore. Everyone seems to lead such busy lives, that there is no longer the time necessary to *be* elegant. Having said that, every once in awhile I try pamper my family and serve them an extravagent dish!

Ingredients:

8 oz. cream cheese at room temperature
10 oz. sour cream
2 eggs lightly beaten
2 tbl chopped white of scallion
½ cup chopped fresh dill
1 lb crab meat
White ground pepper
Salt, if needed
1½ stick sweet butter melted
4 tsp chopped shallots
1½ lb cleaned mushrooms, finely chopped
1 box of filo dough

Preheat oven to 350°. Mix the cream cheese until smooth, gradually adding sour cream. Add eggs, scallions, fresh dill, crab and salt and pepper to taste. Cook shallots in a bit of melted butter until transparent. Add a little more butter and sauté the mushrooms over medium-high heat until nearly all liquid is evaporated. Place mushrooms, shallots, and crab mixture into a greased 10x15-inch oval casserole. Top with as many individually buttered sheets of filo as desired and place a rose fashioned of filo in the center. Bake at 350°, 35-40 minutes.

SALMON CAPERS

Pasta is popular! This recipe has the nutrition of salmon, the capers of hors d'ourves, the dill and cream of a fine soup – all in one dish.

Ingredients:
2 cups heavy cream
4 tbl sweet butter
7 tsp salt
Pinch of freshly grated nutmeg
1 lb. of fresh spinach pasta
1 tbl grated imported parmesan cheese
1½ - 2 cups flaked poached salmon, all skin and bones removed
1/3 cup chopped fresh dill, plus additional dill sprigs for garnish
1 tbl capers

Bring the cream and half of the butter to a simmer in a small saucepan. Add 1 tsp of the salt, and the nutmeg, continue to simmer until the cream is reduced by about one third. Bring 4 quarts water to a boil in a large pot, add remaining 2 tsp of salt and drop in the noodles. (Just 2 -3 minutes should do it.) Meanwhile, stir grated Parmesan then the flaked salmon and ½ cup chopped dill into the cream and remove from heat.

Drain the pasta, return it to the hot pan and toss with remaining butter and capers until butter is melted. Divide pasta equally among 6 heated plates and spoon salmon cream sauce over each portion. Garnish with a sprig of fresh dill and serve immediately.

WESTERN STEAK AND SAUSAGE

There is nothing like an old-fashioned, stick-to-your-ribs meal. My western pal Bill's version of a French cassoulet is savory, hearty and delicious!

Ingredients:
½ lb. Steak, round or sirloin, cut in cubes
½ lb. Ground pork sausage
1 can 14.5 - 15 oz. Red kidney beans, drained and rinsed
1 can 14.5 – 15 oz. Pinto beans or Great Northern Whites, drained and rinsed
1 can 14.5 – 15 oz. Black Beans, drained and rinsed
1 can 14.5 –15 oz. tomato sauce
12 – 14 oz. of your favorite salsa (Bill says it is best to use chunky)
2 cups water
1 – 2 tbl chili powder
Salt and fresh black ground black pepper to taste

Brown the sausage in a dutch oven or a heavy skillet. Remove sausage from the dutch oven/skillet with a slotted spoon to save drippings; set aside; cook steak in drippings until brown; remove and drain well; return sausage to dutch oven; add all your beans, tomato sauce, water, chili powder and salsa. Bring to a boil, reduce heat and simmer, covered, 1½ hours, stirring occasionally. When cooked through, serve with red chili biscuits, sourdough bread or tortillas.

OSSO BUCO MILANESE

This tempting treat is a recipe supplied by my Italian friend, Lynn. Delizioso, Lynn!

Ingredients:
6 veal shanks
½ cup flour
1/3 cup olive oil and 3 tbsp butter
1 medium onion, finely chopped
1 carrot, finely chopped
1 celery stock, finely chopped
2-3 tbl garlic, finely chopped
½ cup dry white wine (or canned beef stock)
6–8 cups tomato sauce (recipe below)
2 tbl Italian parsley, chopped
Salt and freshly ground black pepper to taste

Dust veal shanks with flour and pat off excess. Heat oil and butter in heavy oven–proof casserole until smoking (careful not to burn); add veal to casserole and brown on all sides. (Lynn says not to move the veal around too much or you will not get a good crust.) Get one side well browned before turning. Remove meat to bowl and add onions to casserole pan and brown. Add carrot; brown; add garlic and sauté briefly; add wine or stock and deglaze the pan getting all the bits from the bottom of the pot up. Season with salt and freshly cracked pepper. Replace veal in casserole and add tomato sauce just to below top of veal and bring to a bubble. Cover casserole and lower heat to a simmer. Cook 1½ - 2 hours or until meat is tender. (Can be done a day ahead – Lynn says it usually tastes better when done this way.) Next day: remove casserole from refrigerator and heat in a 350°

oven 30-45 minutes or until meat and sauce are well cooked. Arrange on platter and sprinkle with parsley.

Side Dishes:
MR. OSAKA'S BEAN SPROUTS

In episode #105 (*Mr. Osaka's Tree*), the family nurtured a Bonsai tree given to them by Mr. Osaka. We hoped that it would not die just as we held out optimism for Mr. Osaka himself. Our producer, Ed Hartmann, had a great fondness for Asian culture and several of our episodes and characters reflected that affection. In tribute to Mr. Hartmann, here is a lovely bean sprout dish my family has enjoyed for years.

Ingredients:
2 tbl sesame oil
2 tsp sesame seeds
½ bean sprouts
2 tbls soy sauce
¼ lb mushrooms*
1/3 small can water chestnuts, sliced

Heat oil in skillet. Add seeds and sauté until just brown. Add sprouts and stir. When sprouts soften, add soy sauce, prepared mushrooms and water chestnuts. Toss to mix the flavors and serve hot.

*To prepare mushrooms, place in a small skillet and cook until moisture has evaporated and the pan is dry; then add to the sprouts.

**Cissy says: For a simpler dish, omit the mushrooms, water chestnuts and sesame seeds. Be certain to use the sesame oil because it is waaaay better than any other oil for this dish. Sayonara!

PARTY SKINS

Sometimes I need something a little different to serve for a Sunday afternoon of watching football or having friends over for cocktails. This recipe is easy, tasty and can enhance almost any casual occasion.

Ingredients:
2¼ lb red potatoes
3 tbl olive oil
Salt
HAM AND CHEESE SAUCE
1 tbl butter
1 tbl all-purpose flour
1¼ cups milk
½ cup shredded Cheddar cheese (2 oz.)
1/3 cup minced cooked ham
Pinch of red cayenne pepper

Cut unpeeled potatoes lengthwise into even wedges. Cook in boiling water 5 minutes then drain. Preheat oven to 425°. Cool potato wedges until able to handle (no hot potatoes here!), then cut out the centers, leaving about ½-inch shells. Place skins on a baking sheet and brush with oil, then sprinkle with salt. Bake about 20 minutes, until crisp.

Meanwhile make the SAUCE. Melt butter in a small saucepan. Stir in flour, and then gradually add in milk. Cook, stirring constantly, until thickened. Stir in cheese and ham. Continue stirring until cheese melts, and season with cayenne. Serve warm with potato skins.

CEVICHE

This Mexican fish dish is a favorite from my sister Beverly in La Jolla (Southern California). It has become very popular in restaurants over the last several years, but I enjoy her recipe the best!

Ingredients:
½ bay scallops or white fish
½ cup fresh lemon juice
½ tsp cumin
2 tbl chopped tomatoes
1 tbl chopped red onion
¼ cup salsa
1 tbl chopped cilantro

Marinate the fish in lemon juice for one hour in the refrigerator. Mix with salsa, cumin, chopped tomatoes, chopped cilantro and chopped onion. Serve as a first course with guacamole and taco chips.

SOUTHWEST SLAW

The following recipes are from my friend Bronco Bill, whom I met at the Tombstone Arizona Film Festival and who taught my urban son about cowboys!

Ingredients:
1 medium head green cabbage (shredded) or 1 1-lb package of pre cut
1 medium onion, sliced
1 medium green bell pepper chopped
1 cup white vinegar

¾ cup salad oil
1 cup sugar
1 tsp celery seed
Salt to taste (1 tsp more or less)

Shred cabbage or put pre-cut, pre-packaged mix in a large salad bowl. Place in layers, cabbage, onion and green bell pepper. Top with 1 cup of sugar. Mix remaining ingredients and place in a saucepan and bring to a boil. Remove from heat and pour over cabbage mixture immediately. Cover and place in refrigerator. Let stand 6–8 hours (better 2–3 days!) Serve with your favorite cowboy grub dish.

ARIZONA COWBOY CAVIAR

My son loves this dish, which is really a spiced-up version of black-eyes peas!

Ingredients:
2 cans (15.5-16 oz.) Black-eyed peas, rinsed and drained
½ cup Red wine vinegar
1/3 cup Salad Oil
1 onion, minced (about ¼ cup)
1 tbsp Green chilies, seeded and minced
1 large clove garlic, crushed
½ tsp salt
½ tsp sugar
¼ tsp fresh ground pepper
½ tsp Tabasco sauce
¼ tsp Tabasco green pepper sauce
Chopped pimento for garnish

Mix well black-eyed peas, vinegar, oil, onion, green chilies, garlic, salt, sugar and pepper. Cover and refrigerate for 2 days or up to two weeks before serving. Drain, add garnish. Serve a portion on a small plate with a side fork or put on a slice of sourdough bread.

POTATO PANCAKES

This is the one recipe upon which Geoffrey Mark and I disagreed. My recipe has more of a cowboy, western flair to it. Geoff's is his great-grandmother's Jewish recipe from Russia. For your approval, here are both recipes:

KATHY'S KOWBOY POTATO PANCAKES

Ingredients:
1½ lbs raw potatoes, peeled
2½ tbl flour
1 tsp salt
2 eggs, beaten
3 slices bacon, diced (optional)
1 onion minced
Shortening

Grate potatoes and drain off juice, add the remaining ingredients to the potatoes and mix well. In a pan, heat just enough shortening to make ¼ inch. The shortening should be sizzling hot. Drop the potato mixture from a spoon into the hot fat. Fry the pancake batter, turning once, until golden brown on both sides. Dry on absorbent paper towel and serve with applesauce or sour cream.

GEOFFREY'S POTATO LATKES

Ingredients:
8 russet potatoes, peeled
3 eggs
2 or 3 cups matzoh meal
3 brown onions
Kosher salt and black pepper to taste
Extra virgin olive oil
1 pint sour cream
Caviar
1 package onion soup mix
¼ cup grated Romano cheese

Finely grate peeled potatoes and peeled onions in a food processor until creamy but not liquefied. Add the eggs while processing. Pour mixture into a large bowl and slowly add the matzoh meal, making sure that the batter has the consistency of oatmeal and is neither too runny nor too thick. Add more meal if needed to thicken, or an extra egg if too thick. Add salt and pepper to taste.

    In a large skillet, add at least an inch of oil and heat until a bit of water dropped in forms balls. Using a ladle, spoon in just enough batter to make a small pancake. Brown the pancakes on one side and turn, browning the other side. Note that as you fry more pancakes, the faster the frying will go, so be careful not to burn them. Add more oil to the pan as needed to keep the frying consistent. Lay a paper towel on a plate and dry the first pancakes as they are done; cover them with another paper towel. Continue to add pancakes and layers of toweling until the entire batter is fried. Allow the pancakes to cool slightly and drain. Mix the sour cream, the onion soup mix and the Romano cheese until creamy. Remove the pancakes from the toweling, put on a lovely platter and serve with the sour cream mixture and black caviar. For those with less cultivated palates, serve applesauce!

NOODLE PUDDING

This Eastern-European favorite is made with varying ingredients depending upon from which part of Europe ones ancestors came. It is sometimes referred to as *Luction Kugle*. My co-author Geoffrey Mark remembers his mother making this with pineapple; I was taught to use apples. This recipe came from my friend Janet.

Ingredients:
1 lb broad noodles
¾ stick unsalted margarine, melted
6 eggs beaten
1 tbl brown sugar
4 granny smith apples, peeled and sliced
¾-1 cup raisins
1 cup chopped walnuts
1 cup chopped dried apricots
Margarine
Cinnamon to taste

Preheat oven to 350°. Cook noodles until tender (Janet says not to overcook). Add all ingredients and gently mix. Grease a Pyrex dish 13x9x2. Add mixture and dot with pieces of margarine. Bake 35-40 minutes until golden brown. You might want to cover it lightly if the top of the pudding starts to brown too quickly.

Desserts, Breads, and Snacks:

HIP HERMITS

This is a "happening" little treat that we have enjoyed for years. It is easy to make and delicious!

Ingredients:

½ cup margarine
3/4 cup granulated sugar
½ cup dark brown sugar
1 egg
¼ cup molasses
5 3/4 tbl water
3 cups all-purpose flour
1½ tsp baking soda
½ tsp cloves
1 tsp ginger
1 tsp cinnamon
1½ cup raisins

Cream together margarine and sugars. Stir in the egg, molasses and water. In another bowl, combine the flour, baking soda, cloves, ginger, salt, and cinnamon. Add the butter mixture and stir. Stir in the raisins. Chill the dough from 2 to 24 hours. Divide the dough into four equal pieces and roll into 4 sausage shapes with your hands.

    Preheat oven to 350°. Grease two baking sheets with margarine. Place 2 sausage rolls length wise on each baking sheet. Bake 45 minutes; the dough will flatten. Let cool one minute, then cut into pieces while still warm, and place on a wire rack to cool completely. Makes 18 Hermits.

- Kathy Suggests: Don't overcook. Hermits should be moist.

CISSY'S CRANBERRY COULIS OVER SLICED ORANGES

Refreshing, tangy and kicky – this one is a real surprise the first time you try it. We enjoy it as a dessert after a hearty meal, with lunch or brunch or as an adjunct to cocktails and bridge.

Ingredients:
1½ lb. fresh cranberries
1¼ cup sugar
1 cup fresh orange juice
Grated zest of 1 orange
½ cup water
1/3 cup orange liqueur (Mr. French used Grand Marnier)
6 oranges (without peel or membranes), cut into ½-inch slices.

In a medium-size saucepan simmer the cranberries, sugar and orange juice without a cover for about 15 minutes. Add the orange zest and water and simmer uncovered another 15 minutes, stirring occasionally. Strain the cranberry mixture through a sieve. Stir in the liqueur. Let cool to room temperature. Take out 6 small plates, and put a dollop of the cranberry mixture on each dish. Fan out a sliced orange on each cranberry pool; put more cranberry Coulis over the top of the oranges.

CAT CAKES

This is a great Halloween treat, because you can make them as sweet and as spooky as you like!

Ingredients:
1 cup self-rising flour
¼ cup unsweetened cocoa powder
½ cup margarine, softened
3/4 cup packed light brown sugar
2 eggs, beaten,
2 tbl milk

DECORATIONS:
1 cup powdered sugar, sifted
6 tbl butter, softened
Chocolate buttons
Gumdrops, licorice strands and candies.

Preheat oven to 350°. Put all the cake ingredients into a medium-sized bowl and beat until smooth. Divide cake batter evenly among 20 paper cupcake liners placed in 2 muffin pans. Place water in unused cups. Bake about 15 minutes, until firm to the touch. Cool on a wire rack. Trim tops to flatten if there are peaks.

To decorate, beat powdered sugar and butter together until light and fluffy in a small bowl. Spread over tops of cakes. Attach 2 chocolate buttons on each cake for ears, and place a gumdrop for the nose. Cut slices of licorice candies to make eyes. Cut piece of licorice strand to make whiskers and insert 3 on each side of candy nose.

Meooowwwww!
Here are a few recipes from some "sweet" friends:

MICHELLE'S ULTIMATE BARS

Ingredients:
2 ¼ cups all-purpose flour
1 tsp baking soda
1 tsp salt
2 sticks butter or margarine
¾ cup dark brown sugar
¾ cup granulated sugar
2 eggs
1 tsp vanilla extract
2 cups white baking chips
½ cup macadamia nuts, chopped
½ cup shredded coconut (preferably unsweetened)

Preheat oven to 375°. In medium-sized bowl combine flour, baking soda and salt. Set aside. In large bowl, cream the butter and sugars. Add the eggs and vanilla, beating well. Add the flour mixture, stirring until well blended. Stir in the white baking chips, nuts and coconut. Spread batter in baking sheet approximately 15"x 10". Aluminum foil baking sheets work best. Bake for 25 minutes or until golden. Cool.

LATSON'S DEEP SOUTH PECAN PIE

It almost seems superfluous to introduce a recipe for pecan pie. It is an American classic, served seemingly everywhere. Not all of us had Southern grandmothers to pass down recipes: this is for you.

Ingredients:
1 stick butter
½ cup sugar
¾ cup Karo syrup (white)
¼ cup Maple syrup
3 eggs (slightly beaten)
1 cup chopped pecans
1 cup pecan halves
1 tsp vanilla
Unbaked 9" pie shell
Whipped cream

Cream butter well. Add sugar slowly creaming until light. Slowly stir in syrups, eggs, vanilla and 1 cup broken pecan pieces. Pour into shell; top with pecan halves. Bake at 350° for 55 minutes or until set. Serve cold or warm with whipped cream and a dash of cinnamon.

CHOCOLATE LAYER BARS

Chocolate; just the word itself brings a smile to my face and the stirring of saliva to my mouth. Chocolate and rum? Superb, sensual, sinful and singularly satisfying!

Filling Ingredients:
I package 12 oz. semi-sweet chocolate chips
8 oz. cream cheese
1 can evaporated milk (6.3 oz. can)
1 cup of chopped walnuts
1 tsp rum extract

Step One: Put chocolate chips, cream cheese and milk in a pot, melt it down. Add the walnuts and rum extract.

Bar Ingredients:
3 cups of flour
1½ cups of sugar
1 tsp baking powder
½ tsp of salt
1 cup of softened butter
2 eggs
1 tsp rum extract

Step Two: Mix all of the above very well in a large bowl. Put ½ of Step Two in a 12 ½" x 9" baking pan. Add the filling (Step One) in a layer then add the other half of Step Two. Bake in a 375° oven for 50 minutes.

CRANBERRY UPSIDE-DOWN CAKE

Cranberries were once limited to Thanksgiving Dinner and the occasional juice drink. In the 1980s, suddenly cranberries were everywhere as people discovered their nutritional value and just how darn appetizing they were when not stuck in a jelly next to a slab of dry turkey. Soon, recipes included them in everything from omelets to martinis. This is my version of the classic pineapple cake with a new twist!

Ingredients:
¾ cup butter or margarine (1½ sticks) softened (divided use)
2/3 cup packed light brown sugar
2 cups fresh or frozen cranberries
½ cup pecans, coarsely chopped
1 ½ cups all-purpose flour
1 tsp baking powder
3 large eggs, separated
1 tsp vanilla extract
½ cup milk

Preheat oven to 350°. Line the inside of a 9-inch spring-form pan with foil. Grease foil. Melt ¼ cup butter and pour into pan; tilt to coat bottom evenly. Sprinkle with brown sugar. Sprinkle with cranberries and pecans, spreading cranberries evenly.

In a medium bowl, stir together flour and baking powder in a small bowl with mixer at medium speed; beat egg whites until foamy; increase speed to medium high and beat until soft peaks form when beaters are lifted. Gradually beat in ¼ cup granulated sugar and again beat until stiff peaks form when beaters are lifted. In large bowl with mixer at low speed, beat remaining ½ cup butter and remaining ¾ cup granulated sugar until blended. Increase speed to medium, beating 2 minutes or until fluffy. Beat in egg yolks until well blended. Beat in vanilla. Reduce speed to low. Beat in flour mixture alternately with milk just until blended. Stir in 1 large spoonful of beaten egg whites. In two additions, fold in remaining white just until blended. Turn batter into prepared pan and spread evenly. Bake 60 to 70 minutes until toothpick inserted in center comes out clean. Cool in pan on wire rack 15 minutes. Invert cake onto cake plate and remove side of pan and foil. Cool completely.

BURIED TREASURE MUFFINS

I must admit there are days when there is just no time for breakfast or lunch. While there are many fine muffins on the market (and the Hostess and Drake's products have been comfort food for two generations), I'd rather make my own and be in control of both the freshness and inclusion of ingredients.

Ingredients:
1½ cups all-purpose flour
½ cup sugar
1 cup fresh or frozen blueberries
2½ tsp baking powder
1 tsp ground cinnamon
½ tsp salt
1 egg beaten
2/3 cups buttermilk
½ cups butter or margarine, melted
3 tbl peach preserves

Topping:
1 tsp sugar
¼ tsp ground cinnamon

Preheat oven to 400°. Line 12 medium muffin cups with paper liners, and set aside. Combine flour, ½ cup sugar, blueberries, baking powder, 1 tsp cinnamon and salt in medium bowl. Combine egg, buttermilk and butter or margarine in small bowl. Add to flour mixture; mix just until moistened.

Spoon about 1 tbl batter into each muffin cup. Drop a scant tsp of preserves into the center of batter in each cup; top with remaining batter. Combine 1 tsp sugar and 1 tsp cinnamon in small bowl, sprinkle evenly over tops of batter. Bake 18 - 20 minutes or lightly browned. Remove muffin to wire rack to cool completely.

SOPHISTICATED SCONES

The Irish side of me really enjoys these not-too-sweet treats with afternoon tea, especially after a recording session.

Ingredients:
1 1/3 cup flour
½ tsp baking soda
½ tsp cream of tartar
¼ tsp salt
3 tsp sugar
1/3 cup cold butter
1/3 cup milk
3 tbl raisins

Pre heat oven to 450°. Mix together the flour, soda, cream of tartar, salt and sugar. Cut in the butter and add milk to make a soft dough. Add raisins. Knead lightly and roll out. Cut with biscuit cutter and place on greased cookie sheet. (You can also drop the batter by the tsp.) Bake for 6 minutes or until light brown.

MARVELOUS MADELEINES

Although this recipe has many small steps, once you have done it, it will seem like a piece of cake (or a cookie!). I love the buttery, almond flavor, especially when the pastry is still warm!

Ingredients:
7 oz. almond paste, cut into small pieces
1 cup granulated sugar
5 eggs room temperature
1 tsp almond extract
2 tsp orange-flower water
1 cup sifted unbleached all-purpose flour
1 tsp baking powder
10 tbl (1¼ sticks) unsalted butter, melted and cooled
Confectioner's sugar for dusting

Cream the almond paste and granulated sugar in a food processor fitted with a steel blade or with a heavy duty mixer fitted with a paddle. Transfer to a large mixing bowl and add the eggs, one at a time, beating well after each addition. Add the almond extract and the orange-flower water and beat until light and fluffy, 1-2 minutes. Sift the flour and baking powder together and gently fold into the almond mixture. Gently fold in the melted butter just until combined. Refrigerate the batter for 1 hour.

Preheat the over to 400°. Brush Madeleine molds with melted butter and dust lightly with flour. Spoon the batter into the molds, filling them three-fourths full. Bake until lightly colored, 8-to-10 minutes. Let cool for 5 minutes and then gently remove to wire racks to cool completely. Allow the molds to cool before re-brushing with melted butter and repeating the process with the remaining batter. Dust with confectioner's sugar before serving.

BLUEBERRY STREUSEL TEA BREAD

It's nice to remember that there actually was a time when ladies would get together and have leisurely tea parties -- who has time for that with today's hectic lifestyle? For those of you who still like gracious living, or just want a wonderful concoction to serve with Sunday brunch, please try this tea bread!

Ingredients:
2½ cups all-purpose flour
1½ tsp baking powder
½ tsp baking soda
½ tsp salt
½ cup butter or margarine (1 stick) softened
1¼ cups sugar
1 tsp vanilla extract
2 large eggs
1 (8 oz.) container sour cream
1 ½ cups fresh or frozen blueberries

Streusel:
¼ cup all-purpose flour
¼ cup packed light brown sugar
1 tbsp chopped pecans
1/8 tsp ground cinnamon
1 tbsp better or margarine, softened

Preheat oven to 350°. Grease a 9x5-inch metal loaf pan, dust with flour. In medium bowl, stir together flour, baking powder, baking soda and salt. In a large bowl, with mixer at low speed, beat butter until smooth. Add sugar, beat until creamy. Beat in vanilla.

Reduce speed to low and add eggs, one at a time, beating after each addition until well blended, scraping bowl occasionally with rubber spatula. Add flour mixture alternately with sour cream, beginning and ending with flour mixture. Fold in blueberries.

For Streusel topping:

With fingertips, mix ingredients until blended. Spoon batter into prepared loaf pan. Sprinkle streusel over batter. Bake about 40 minutes or until a toothpick inserted into the loaves come out clean.

CHEESY FARM ANIMALS

Whether you are a parent, grandparent or just have children in your life, one can never be too careful about the foods they eat. This nutritious snack is fun to make and fun to eat.

Ingredients:
1 cup all-purpose flour
½ tsp mustard powder
¼ stick butter, chilled
½ cup shredded sharp Cheddar cheese
1 egg, beaten
Sesame seeds

Preheat oven to 350°. Grease 2 baking sheets. Sift flour and mustard into a bowl. Cut in butter until mixture resembles breadcrumbs. Stir in cheese then add 2 tbl of the beaten egg and mix together to make smooth dough. Turn dough out onto a floured surface and knead lightly. Roll out to about 1-inch thick.

Using animal-shaped cookie cutters, cut out animal crackers, re-rolling trimmings. Place on baking sheets. Brush tops with remaining beaten egg and sprinkle with sesame seeds. Bake 12-15 minutes until golden. Cool on a wire rack.

PEANUT TWIRLS

I have an incredible sweet tooth, especially for a lady who is over for – well, let's put it this way: if you are old enough to have seen *Family Affair* in its original run, I won't tell *your* age if you won't tell *mine*! I much prefer homemade treats to those that are store bought. They are less expensive, and more often than not have better ingredients. This recipe makes a fun snack and gets its sweetness from the peanut butter!

Ingredients:
1½ cup self-rising flour
½ tsp mustard powder
1/3 cup margarine
½ cup unshredded Cheddar cheese
3 tbl milk
Peanut butter
Garnish with lettuce leafs and radish

Preheat oven to 375°. Grease a baking sheet. Sift flour and mustard together into a bowl. Cut in margarine until mixture resembles fine breadcrumbs. Stir in cheese, then milk to make a fairly soft dough.

Turn out the dough onto a flour surface and knead lightly

until smooth. Roll dough into a rope shape about 12 inches long. Cut into 20 equal slices. Roll out each slice into a thin rope shape about 6 inches long. Gently press three quarters of the length to make dough about a half-inch wide. Spread a little peanut butter along the flattened surface, then roll up toward the unflattened end to make a snail shape. Form a head at the end. Transfer to baking sheet. Repeat with remaining dough. Bake 12-15 minutes, until golden. Cool on a wire rack. Serve with lettuce leaves and radish.

Thinking up a new recipe

Brian Keith, Johnny Whitaker, Anissa Jones and I pose for the camera during our fourth season.

Mr. French and the kids react to a phone call from Uncle Bill.

The fifth season finds the family attending an intriguing art exhibit.

Legendary Myrna Loy around the time she appeared on our show.

Two-time guest star Ida Lupino and our own Sebastian Cabot smile as they take direction from Charles Barton, who is unseen.

Handsome Robert Reed guested with us before his *Brady Bunch* fame.

Brian's birthday during fifth season

Cooking Up a Good Show: They Made It All Possible

A discussion of *Family Affair* would not be complete without a huge tip of the hat to the people who made it all possible. It starts with Don Fedderson and Ed Hartmann. Without them, there would have been no Cissy or Mr. French, there would have been no Chip or Ernie on *My Three Sons*, and without Don there might not have even been a Johnny Carson on *The Tonight Show*.

Don Fedderson (1913-1994) was one of television's most prolific producers. While he did not own a studio like Lucille Ball and Desi Arnaz, he personally produced almost as many hit shows that remain television classics. Don got his start in local Los Angeles television at a time when there were probably more technicians on the set then there were viewers who *owned* sets! It was he who realized the great talent that neophyte Betty White possessed, and helped her make the transition from local television hostess to Emmy-winning television star by producing her first series, *Life with Elizabeth*. When that show ran its course, he again showed his flair for recognizing television talent and helped produce the long-running *Lawrence Welk Show*.

Never one to rest on his laurels, he brought the great comedian Edgar Bergen to the quiz-show format with *Do You Trust Your Wife?* When that show was transferred to daytime television a couple of seasons later (and renamed *Who Do You Trust?*), Johnny Carson took over as host. It was here that Johnny was first paired with jolly Ed McMahon and where America really fell in love with them both. It was no wonder that they were later tapped to host *The Tonight Show* for an incredible thirty-year run.

Betty White was never far from Don's mind, and he sold a revised version of *Life with Elizabeth* (called *Date with the Angels*) to ABC. This was his least successful show. He had no worries, because he was also producing *The Millionaire*, which had a healthy six-season run.

I had appeared on *The Millionaire* when I was a child. That was an experience I won't forget! I had dutifully learned all my lines; however, I didn't learn the cues. Once I got started on the first word I knew where I was in the dialogue, but I didn't know when to say them! A quick coaching on the set got me through, but I didn't work for Mr. Fedderson on any more of his shows under I was cast in *Family Affair*.

Fedderson's next foray into the world of situation comedy brought him untold riches. He wanted to do a show about the trials and tribulations of an all-male household. The concept included a middle-aged father, his blustery father-in-law, and his three sons, aged ten to eighteen. Many big name actors were considered for the role of the father, but none of them suited Don's sense of responsibility coupled with a flair for comedy. His first choice, Fred MacMurray, wouldn't do the show.

MacMurray, well into middle age, had recently had a boon to his career with a series of comedy films for Walt Disney where he played nice but bungling men. These films, along with a career that spanned back into the late 1920s on stage and on screen, left Fred wealthy and lazy. In those days, sitcoms ran for thirty-nine shows a season with only thirteen weeks off. Mr. MacMurray did not want to work that hard, nor did he want to abandon motion pictures.

Rising to the challenge, Don Fedderson developed a unique way of shooting what became the TV series, *My Three Sons*. Fred would only work thirteen weeks a year, filming all of his scenes in all of the episodes first. Then the rest of the cast would film the remainder of the scenes for all of the episodes without him, and the result would be seamlessly edited together. Under these circumstances, MacMurray agreed to do the show.

My Three Sons ran until 1972, adding wives and girlfriends played by such favorites as Beverly Garland and Tina Cole. The show was still doing well in the ratings when it was cancelled to make room for newer and more adult product. Twelve seasons of shows made Don Fedderson a fortune!

While *My Three Sons* was filming, Don Fedderson added Family Affair to his rich TV palette. Don made the same deal with Brian Keith that he had offered Fred MacMurray. When casting director Virginia Martindale called me to interview for a new series, my mother came to pick me up at UCLA to take me on the audition. We had been told the production team was looking for a blonde-haired teenager to play the part of "Cissy"; the other parts had already been cast and they were starting to film the pilot the next week.

My mother, ever inventive, bought a can of Streaks and Tips (a colored hairspray no longer on the market that could -- well, temporarily - add colored streaks to your hair) and sprayed my hair to lighten my dark locks to a golden sheen. The intelligent and warm-natured Ed Hartmann (for whom I always had great affection) interviewed me. Ed (1911-2003) had been a screenwriter for films as far back as 1936 and had been the president of the Writers Guild from 1955-59. His association with Don Fedderson as a co-producer and co-creator made a huge difference on the quality of the many series they did together. While we were chatting, he did a double take.

"What's wrong with your hair?" he said. "My hair?" I replied. "Yes," he said. "It's turning green!" The boy with green hair not withstanding, my face turned red -- I'm sure it was quite a colorful picture in front of him! After viewing a tape of the TV show *Death Valley Days*, where I starred as a young Isadora Duncan opposite June Lockhart, the powers that be decided I might have the acting chops to fill the shoes of "Catherine Patterson Davis" on their new show *Family Affair*. Happily, it was decided that I should do a screen test on the set where they were filming the pilot at Desilu Studios next to the Paramount lot in Hollywood.

I was advised to go to Max Factor in Hollywood, the premier makeup and wig shop at the time, and pick out a blonde wig. I did and came to the set looking like Alice in Wonderland, complete with a blue-checked dress. I got the job, but was told never to wear that wig again!

Mr. Fedderson rarely came to the set – he watched the dailies of *My Three Sons* and *Family Affair* and then *To Rome with Love* and kept his eye on his realms. John Stephens, the production manager, was one of those stellar professionals who really got the *Family Affair* show on its feet and kept it there. He was in charge of making sure the locations were correct, and had the unenviable job of creating the shooting schedule to fit the star's three-month time frame -- no small task as we would be shooting scenes from perhaps four different shows in one day to meet Brian's deadline. This was a continuity nightmare, but we did it with only a few setbacks. Even when Sebastian Cabot had to miss several shows for surgery on his hand, it was all worked into the schedule so that Brian could shoot his scenes with both Mr. Cabot and John Williams (his temporary replacement) within that thirteen-week time frame.

It was a little more difficult when Anissa Jones broke her leg. You see, they never planned on showing Anissa's break at all. Clever filming, using creative camera angles with well-placed furniture to hide her infirmity, and a double to do the walking where necessary were all planned out. Then little Miss Jones broke her leg a second time, and this time we had no choice. This is the one instance where continuity errors crept into the editing, and Buffy would have a broken leg one week but not the next, and sometimes can be seen walking with and without crutches even in the same episode!

Thelma Strahm, our wardrobe mistress, had to make sure that the entire wardrobe matched from scene to scene, even if those scenes were shot months apart. Our hair stylists had to make the same notes for our hair. Every season Cissy would get a new "official" hairstyle for the entire season. This was done so that no matter which episodes we might be shooting scenes for on the same day, the curls would always match.

I usually liked the clothing provided for Cissy to wear starting with the second year (the first year, we kids supplied our own wardrobes). At times they may have been a little juvenile for Kathy (who was in reality a couple of years older than Cissy), but they suited Catherine Patterson Davis and her wealthy New York circumstances. I did get in some debates with our producers, Don, Ed and Fred Henry. It was the sixties!! I wanted miniskirts like they wore on *Laugh-In*! It was decided, however, to employ a classic look and this proved to be a very wise decision. When the shows are viewed today, they are not dated as are some shows from that explosive era.

Only a couple times did I borrow a few things from the show to wear to a party and forget to bring them back the next day. One time a necklace had to be worn on a particular day and it couldn't be found; Thelma did her best to improvise! In the episode where Cissy wanted to be a hippie, the medallion I wore on a chain magically changes from one scene to the next!

Our script writers had a much different and more difficult task than most. Due to Brian's schedule, our head writers and script supervisors, Austin and Irma Kalish, had to make sure that all the scripts written by themselves and the other writers were finished before the season began; most shows had only five or six scripts written ahead of filming. The Kalishes were and are brilliant writers who turned out scripts for some of the best shows on television. They also produced several hit television series and films.

While we were still filming our show, Fedderson began producing the TV series *To Rome with Love*, and this time his movie star was John Forsythe. This show used the same methods we did, but alas the series only lasted for two seasons. Don's follow-up to this show was *The Smith Family*. Not only did he get Henry Fonda to star, but also Ron Howard made his first steps toward acting adulthood on this series, and Don's son, Mike Minor, sang the theme song. This show was another two-season entry. Don Fedderson produced some more pilots for new series and a few made-for-TV movies, but television had drastically changed since he first began producing. Wisely, he retired.

Many people added their special ingredients to make *Fam-*

ily Affair a successful TV series. From the executive producers to the stand-ins – the attention and good humor surrounding the set translated to the screen. Viewers kept returning for more helpings of this tasty TV treat.

The success of the show, I believe, was due to a variety of factors. Number one was the great chemistry between the lead actors and the meshing of various backgrounds:

Brian Keith (1921-1997) was a successful movie actor who had starred in such Westerns as *The Mountain Men* and *The Hallelujah Trail*, as well as other distinguished movies such as *The Parent Trap* with Maureen O'Hara and Hayley Mills, *Reflections in a Golden Eye* with Elizabeth Taylor and *Krakatoa East of Java*, where he met his third wife, Victoria. He brought a rugged manliness to his role as Uncle Bill that was tempered by his innate sensitivity and warmth toward children. His acting approach was natural and expressed from the inside out. For his excellent longevity in the entertainment world, Brian was recently award a star on the Walk of Fame in Hollywood. I was honored to make a speech on his behalf!

It saddens me to mention that his personal life had its share of tragedies. His first son died in childhood. After Brian was diagnosed with emphysema and terminal lung cancer, his beautiful daughter Daisy committed suicide. Wracked with pain and knowing his time was short, Brian called me one day to say goodbye and that he could not bear the physical or emotional pain. Ten weeks after Daisy ended her life, Brian did the same. I feel his loss to this day.

Sebastian Cabot (1918-1977) was a well-respected character actor who had appeared in such films as *Seven Thieves*, and starred in his own series, *The Beachcomber* and *Checkmate*. He brought to the *Family Affair* set an acting style where the character was developed from the outside in and then expressed. Sebastian toiled over his lines to have them letter-perfect – true to the script writer's words. He also had a family whom he adored and a great voice that he used to excellent effect in such Disney animated films as the *Jungle Book* and *Winnie the Pooh*. The two differing acting approaches of Brian and Sebastian created an interesting and very watchful relationship on the show where Sebastian became one of the first TV "nannies." He passed away from a stroke when he was not yet sixty, leaving his wife Kay and three children behind.

When I was cast in *Family Affair*, I already had a vast background in acting in film (*The Ten Commandments*), television (once, I did an episode of Brian's series *The Crusader* in the fifties), radio (*Whispering Streets* with Bette Davis) and stage. Coming from a family of four children with doting parents, I stepped right into one of TV's first dysfunctional families and made it my own. Because I was eighteen (and the children on the show could only work a set number of hours, Brian had limited time and Sebastian was not always in the best of health), I became the workhorse actor on the set. I would arrive at 6:30 A.M. and stay to pick up my close-ups at the end of the day. Many times I did those close-ups opposite our assistant director John Gaudioso, a cigar-smoking and warm but gruff Italian – whom I had to imagine as cute pig-tailed Buffy! Ah, the wonders of imaginative acting!

Anissa Jones (1958-1976) had acted in a few commercials, but the part of Buffy on *Family Affair* was her first big role. She was very intelligent and a natural actress – much in the vein of Brian's acting. Relishing her time off from working and living at the beach in Southern California, she went with abandon into the sea and the pool – unfortunately breaking her leg on one such excursion and causing the production problems I have already shared. Anissa enjoyed the first few years on the show. She had an abundance of talent, and liked making friends with the guests who appeared and excelling in the faux-classroom set up at the studio under the terrific tutelage of our welfare worker, Mrs. Catherine Deeney. Johnny was six when he made our pilot, Anissa was almost eight and was more mature than her reel twin. Johnny was raucous, having come from a family of seven siblings; Anissa had one brother, Paul, and was used to a quieter household.

By the time we wrapped *Family Affair*, Anissa was thirteen, but still playing Buffy as if she were nine and carrying around Mrs. Beasley. One can see from some of her later performances that she was not as happy as in the first years the show was filmed.

It breaks my heart whenever I think of Anissa after our show left the air. She had been under a great deal of stress from performing and from being whisked away each weekend for publicity appearances. Not finding her identity in those crucial pre-teen years and expected to act much younger then her years, took its emotional toll. Anissa was offered the starring part of "Reagan" in the classic thriller *The Exorcist* after *Family Affair* but turned it down. She was done: she had quit show business. She bonded with local teenage friends and started to have the freedom that had been denied her the five years she was on the TV series. Unfortunately those whom she called friends were drug users. Whatever the underlying cause, Anissa masked her pain with proffered drugs. When officials found her body in 1976 she had ingested a combination of cocaine, angel dust, Seconal and Quaaludes. The coroner said it was one of the most massive overdoses he had ever recorded. It was such a tragedy that this amazing little girl, such a bright light, was extinguished at such a young age. Her brother, Paul, also died from an overdose. I shall always remember Anissa as a warm, generous, giving person whom I miss to this day.

Johnny Whitaker (1959 -) was born to a Mormon family with seven siblings. Johnny had met Brian Keith on the set of the movie *The Russians are Coming, the Russians are Coming* and Mr. Keith recommended the red tousled-headed imp for the role of Jody. Younger than Anissa, he had a more difficult time with his lines, but we had an excellent dialogue coach who helped him learn them and cured him of his slight habit of pronouncing the letter L as "aw." In some of the early episodes, it sounds as if Jody is calling out for Uncle Bee-oow. He and Anissa were an adorable pair. When *Family Affair* ended its run, Johnny went on to do guest shots on other shows and had a Saturday morning series in the 1970s, *Sigmund and the Sea Monsters*. After a couple of Disney movies, he went to college and then on a Mormon mission to Portugal. After a short-lived marriage he, like Anissa, became involved in drugs, lost his money, and floundered. His family did an intervention and rescued him and he now counsels others on the dangers of substance abuse and conducts drug interventions.

John Williams (1903–1983) was a Tony Award-winning stage actor and film character actor who was a favorite of Alfred Hitchcock's. On television, he did everything from heavy drama on *Playhouse 90* to slapstick comedy on *The Lucy Show*. No matter what he played, I never saw him give anything less than a wonderful and believable performance. I loved him when he played the role of Audrey Hepburn's father in the classic movie *Sabrina* and I was so excited he joined our cast. John Williams was a dream; he had a nervous sort of personality with a sprinkling of insecurity (it is always difficult coming into a part that has been established by someone else), but he had a tremen-

Funny Lady Nancy Walker joined us for the last season of *Family Affair*.

dous amount of warmth, caring and a great big dollop of talent. It was a heart-rendering farewell when he left us, but Sebastian hastened his recovery to reclaim his role!

Nancy Walker (1922-1992) was hired for our fifth and last season to play Emily Turner, a very down-to-earth cleaning woman who was supposed to free Mr. French from the heavy scrubbing. The character's uneducated, common but heart-of-gold qualities were meant as sparring opportunities for Mr. French's formal and sophisticated airs. Emily was never as fleshed-out a character as the rest of us; they even used the old wheeze about her being a scrubwoman so she could put her handsome son through medical school. Naturally, he developed a crush on Cissy!

Nancy was a seasoned comedienne from Broadway and movies and the producers thought she would be an excellent foil for the proper Mr. French. She did provide new comedic situations and reactions, but I don't think our show was her cup of tea. She told me that the style of her comedy was so different than that of our show that she had to greatly adjust her timing. She was accustomed to fast-paced dialogue; our show was much gentler and slower paced with long reaction times and long-lasting close ups. I actually think she was glad when she was only on the show one season; she was anxious to get back to her fast-paced delivery and comedy. Busy Nancy was also playing Rhoda's mother on *The Mary Tyler Moore Show* and making the first of her many Bounty paper towel commercials while she was with us.

Her husband, David Craig, was the singer teacher/tutor to many actors. His specialty was taking actors who had little singing training and teaching them how to deliver a song. One of his techniques was to get one to imagine the lyrics were being said to an imaginative partner. Rock Hudson and I were two of his grateful singing graduates!

Charles Barton was our dear director for the last four years of the show. William Russell was the director for the first year, but health problems forbade him from continuing. Charlie had a wonderful history of comedy, having directed Abbot and Costello films and then TV series such as *Amos 'n' Andy, The Gale Storm Show* and ninety episodes of *Dennis the Menace*. He was a leprechaun sort of man – loving, with a style akin to Brian Keith, and the same mischievous twinkle in his eye. Charlie would come to the set in the morning, say, "All right, what are we shooting today?" and improvise it from there! All in all, he kept a good humor and was a great asset to our show.

During the 1960s, television writers were not on the set very often and instead much of their time was spent conjuring new ideas and making revisions. Today, they all hover on the set, making changes every five minutes if the laughs aren't there.

The original concept of our show was to appeal to older audiences who were fans of Brian Keith and Sebastian Cabot. Accordingly, CBS gave us a 9:30 P.M. time slot on Monday evening right after *The Lucy Show* and *The Andy Griffith Show*. Buffy, Jody and Cissy, however, became so popular that the shows became less about Brian's escapades with differing beauties and more about the situations involved in parenting three orphans.

Austin (we called him Rocky) Kalish and his wife Irma wrote many of the scripts and were the story editors. All the scripts had to be finished at the beginning of the season so a stable of writers were employed, including Rita Lakin, Edmund Beloin and Henry Garson (who were co-producers the first year), John McGreevey, and George Tibbles. Usually, one script centered about a particular character in *Family Affair* (Uncle Bill, Mr. French, Cissy, Buffy or Jody – and then there was usually a script about the twins together). These episodes expanded, featured our talented guest stars and made for a wonderful mixture of stories. All in all, the sugar and spice that were added by those who worked on *Family Affair* made it a delicious TV meal!!

Many of the actors and crew I have mentioned were and are good friends of mine.

We shared a history and we are blessed to have shared a special place in the hearts of millions of fans all over the world. We worked extremely hard under sometimes very different and difficult circumstances but we loved our work. We are honored that you do too!

Dick Clark and I after I sang my Christmas novelty song *Lem, the Orphan Reindeer* on *American Bandstand*.

Handsome Dennis Cole, 60's leading man from the TV series *Felony Squad*, was also a friend of mine from appearances we made together on the TV game show *Hollywood Squares*.

Young Hollywood of the 60's dining out: Michael Christian, Dack Rambo and me.

I got to work with a lot of handsome men, and boy did I love it! Here I get to giggle with Peter Duryea.

Sheila and Joe Barbera, Zsa Zsa Gabor, famous impresario James Doolittle, who was my mentor and producing partner and me.

Kathy and Greg Fedderson at a Western celebrity event. Kathy's dress is one she wore on a *Big Valley* episode.

My favorite leading man of the 1960s, my dad!

Cooking Up a Show   167

"My favorite leading men today, my husband and my son!"

Index

Cocktails and Beverages
Champagne Cocktail, 79
Cuba Libre, 83
Daiquiri, 83
Eggnog, 79
Gimlet, 82
Highball, 82
Hot Chocolate, 47
Manhattan, 80
Martini, 79
Old Fashioned, 81
Sidecar, 81
Tom Collins, 82
Whiskey Sour, 80

Appetizers, Salads and Soups
Antipasto, 18
Canapés, 50
Clams Casino, 57
Eggstravaganza (Deviled Eggs), 59
Flaming Spinach Salad, 61
Hearts of Palm Salad, 15
Mr. French's Leek and Sausage Tart, 62
Oysters Rockefeller, 55
Salad Nicoise, 60
Salmon Mousse, 57
Three Onion Soup with Croutons, 63

Main Dishes
Beverly's Veal Scaloppini, 114
Bouillabaisse a la Marseillaise, 6
Chicken Chow Mein, 10
Chicken Marengo, 111
Chicken Mushroom Casserole, 115
Coq Au Vin, 67
Crown Roast of Lamb, 51

Curried Chicken and Rice, 24
Eggs Benedict, 1
Elegant Crab Strudel, 119
Filet of Beef Wellington with Pate de Fois Gras, 38
Fish in Papillote with Tomato Basil Beurre Blanc, 70
Fresh Swordfish with Olivada, 113
Jody's Turkey Wrap, 87
Lobster Newberg, 65
Medallions of Lobster A L 'Estragon, 72
Mr. French's Bagel Pizza, 89
Osso Buco Milanese, 122
Pheasant Under Glass, 66
Pork Chops and Rice, 117
Roast Leg of Lamb, 27
Rock Cornish Game Hens, 48
Salmon Capers, 120
Steak Diane, 31
Steak Tartar, 68
Southern Fried Chicken, 43
Swiss Chard Torta, 118
Tuna Noodle Casserole, 116
Untidy Samuel Sandwiches, 21
Welsh Rarebit, 70
Western Steak and Sausage, 121

Side Dishes

Ants on a Beam, 92
Arizona Cowboy Caviar, 126
Asparagus Soufflé, 34
Blintzes, 36
Celery Victor, 33
Ceviche, 125
Cream of Red Bell Pepper Soup, 106
Creamed Cauliflower and Peas, 15
Geoffrey's Potato Latkes, 128
Green Bean and Onion Ring Casserole, 90
Guacamole, 104
Kathy's Kowboy Potato Pancakes, 127
Kathy's Kucumbers, 103
Lebanese Stuffed Grape Leaves, 12
Limestone Lettuce Salad, 105
Marmalade, 9
Mishy Squishy Mashed Potatoes, 91
Mr. French Fries, 92
Mr. French's Family Yorkshire Pudding, 5
Mr. Osaka's Bean Sprouts, 123
Noodle Pudding, 129
Party Skins, 124
Pate de Legumes, 109
Southwest Slaw, 125
Summer Pasta Salad, 107

Desserts

Applesauce Cake, 46

Bananas Foster, 73
Barquette aux Marrons, 22
Blueberry Streusel Teabread, 140
Buffy's Fave Chocolate Pudding, 94
Buried Treasure Muffins, 137
Cat Cakes, 132
Charlotte Russe, 19
Cheesy Farm Animals, 141
Cherries Jubilee, 75
Chocolate Layer Bars, 135
Cissy's Carmel Apple Cutups, 96
Cissy's Coconut Cookies, 95
Cissy's Cranberry Coulis Over
    Sliced Oranges, 131
Cranberry Upside-Down Cake, 136

Crepes Suzette, 17
Do It Yourself Sundaes, 99
Hip Hermits, 130
Jody's Fave Banana Pudding, 93
Latson's Deep South Pecan Pie, 134
Marvelous Madeleines, 139
Michelle's Ultimate Bars, 133
Mr. French's English Toffee, 98
Pancakes Barbara, 73
Peanut Butter S'Mores, 97
Peanut Twirls, 142
Poached Pears, 74
Sophisticated Scones, 138
Torte Macaroon, 42
Terre Haute Oaty Fruit Surprises, 96

www.ingramcontent.com/pod-product-compliance
Lightning Source LLC
Chambersburg PA
CBHW050759160426
43192CB00010B/1579